Becoming a Husband

I'm privileged that I was given an early copy of this book and that I've known Leann and Mike for many years. The stories, lessons, and wisdom are real. This couple has a most unique human trait: honest transparency. This book clues us in on the issues and how to deal with conflict in a way that can bring better health and true intimacy to our marriages. *Becoming a Husband* will be an excellent read for newlyweds as well as us old-timers.

JONEAL KIRBY, PhD, marriage counselor and author

We've had the privilege of walking alongside Leann and her husband, Mike, through some of life's hardest seasons—infidelity, redemption, and the messy, joyful journey of raising children. Their story is one of God's grace, restoration, and resilience. In *Becoming a Husband* and *Becoming a Wife*, Leann offers wisdom forged over more than thirty-seven years of real marriage—missteps, growth, sins, and victories included. These twenty-one-day journals are deeply rooted in Scripture and honesty, helping men and women prepare not just for a wedding but for a lifetime covenant. If you want to build a marriage that reflects God's purpose and withstands life's trials, start here.

ALAN AND LISA ROBERTSON, speakers and authors of *Desperate Forgiveness*, *A New Season*, and *The Duck Commander Devotional for Couples*

Becoming a Husband is more than a devotional—it's a sacred guide for young men as they embark on the most important earthly relationship they'll ever have. Karen Leann Murphy has beautifully captured the heart of biblical manhood and servant leadership. This twenty-one-day journey is rich with truth and practical wisdom drawn from Scripture and real-life experience.

My wife, Mary, and I have been doing premarital counseling with couples for more than thirty years, and we both agree—this book is going to be a required resource for every couple we walk alongside. It prepares a man to lead not with pride but with purpose. Not with force but with faith. It calls him to be the kind of husband who reflects Christ—not just at the altar but every day after.

I recommend this book to every young man preparing for marriage—and to every parent, mentor, or ministry leader who wants to pass on a legacy of godly manhood. This book will bless marriages before they even begin.

MAC OWEN, global director of Celebrate Recovery

BECOMING

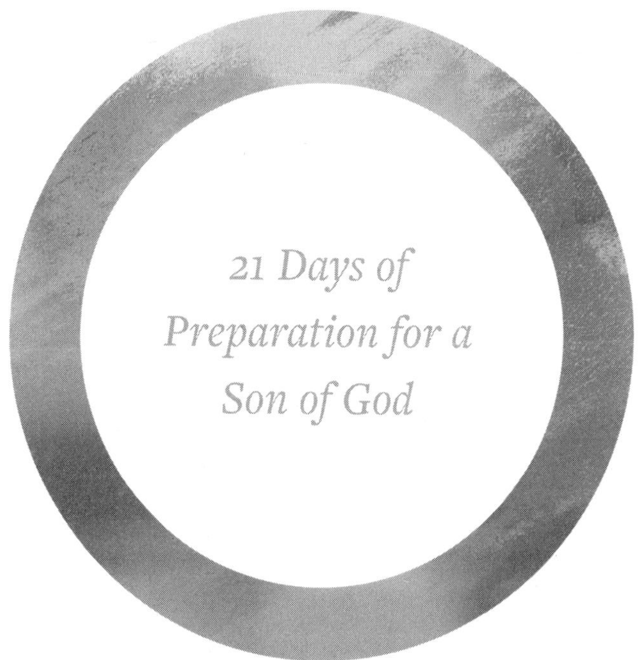

A HUSBAND

KAREN LEANN MURPHY

A Focus on the Family resource
published by Tyndale House Publishers

Becoming a Husband: Twenty-One Days of Preparation for a Son of God

A Focus on the Family book published by Tyndale House Publishers, Carol Stream, Illinois 60188

Edited by Larry Weeden, Andrea Gutierrez, and Sarah Ocenasek

Cover design by Faceout Studio

Interior design by Cathy Miller

For information about special discounts for bulk purchases, please contact Tyndale House Publishers at csresponse@tyndale.com, or call 1-855-277-9400.

ISBN 978-1-64607-205-7

Printed in the United States of America

32 31 30 29 28 27 26
7 6 5 4 3 2 1

He who finds a wife

finds a good thing

and obtains favor from the LORD.

PROVERBS 18:22

For the glory of God, who works all things together

for the good of those who love Him

and are called according to His purpose.

Contents

Introduction

Ever since our sons, Patrick and Colten, were born, my husband, Mike, and I prayed earnestly, first and foremost, that God would draw them to Himself. Second, we prayed that He would bring a wife into each of their lives who would love God far more than Patrick or Colten but no other person as much.

When we brought each boy home from the hospital, their maternal grandmother, Memi, gave him an heirloom handkerchief with a precious poem about how someday it could be given to his wife to carry on her wedding day. And God is faithful. There's no doubt that God answered our prayers with Alexa and Lydia. We love them, and they are both points of joy in our family.

Looking back on our marriage, Mike and I know it would have helped us a lot if we had begun with a better grasp of the work necessary to build a solid marriage, if we had gotten hold of some scriptural and fundamental truths about marriage that are completely counter to the world's view. We really needed someone to offer some suggestions and insights to prepare our hearts and minds for marriage. We found through the years that we didn't have the knowledge needed to be the spouses God called us to be.

In His grace, God has redeemed our sins, mistakes, and failures, but I wish we had fully understood that when you marry, you give up your right to self. We meant our vows, but keeping them seemed so much easier before the wedding than at any point afterward. I hope this book will help you prepare now for those days when putting your wife first seems harder than you can even imagine.

Don't misunderstand; it will still be important for you to take care of yourself and for both of you to have some time for yourselves (as long as you work that out together). However, as God gives your fiancée to you in marriage, your life becomes united with hers—and that's not all romance and joy. Your body belongs to her and hers to you. You're making a covenant of mutual submission.

The world tries to get you to believe a lie about your role—either to buy into the notion that you shouldn't be the leader because that smacks of inequality or that you should be the leader by any means necessary. Both extremes are tools of the enemy. You're called to be a servant-leader like Christ—a servant-leader willing to lay down your life for your wife.

She, in turn, is called to be your *helper*—the same term that's used over and over again to describe God: "Our soul waits for the LORD; he is our help and our shield" (Psalm 33:20); "O God! You are my help and my deliverer" (Psalm 70:5); "You who fear the LORD, trust in the LORD! He is their help and their shield" (Psalm 115:11). This is no inferior role. God chose this woman to be your help as God is your help—one who will assist you in doing what you can't do alone and help you become more than you can on your own.

You must be constantly, intentionally mindful of the role God has given each of you. You must be purposeful in being her partner, her support, her leader in the same sense that Christ leads us—not with force or demands but with love and encouragement.

Both of you are called to seek a supernatural relationship, not to follow the world's pattern of seeking fulfillment of your own needs. In a supernatural marriage, a Christian marriage, two people submit their wills and hearts first to God and then to each other.

I hope you find some help from the things Mike and I have spent more than thirty years of marriage learning (often the hardest way), messing up, repairing, and relearning. We haven't come close to mastering any of this, but we would love to see you skip some of the mistakes we've made and avoid some of the heartbreak we've faced.

You've made the second-most-important decision of your life—to get married—and are rapidly approaching the second-most-important day of your life—your wedding. On the most important day of your life, you made the most important decision of your life, acknowledging Jesus as Lord and Savior and dedicating your life to Him. That commitment to Jesus makes this time in your life even more special, a celebration and a reflection of Christ's love for the church. You're on an exciting countdown to getting married!

This book is written for those men who have chosen Jesus, for sons of God. It flies in the face of what the world believes. To truly live the will of God daily will challenge you. But trust God, live like Jesus, and rely on the strength of the Holy Spirit.

I've written this collection of messages with the hope that you will commit to spending intentional time every day over the three weeks prior to your wedding reading each day's thoughts, writing your answers in the journal section, and then sharing those journal entries with your fiancée. Then I hope you'll return to this journal the month before your first anniversary, revisit each chapter, and spend some time writing anniversary reflections about your growth, challenges, and goals as a husband.

I trust that as you share this book and your thoughts with your fiancée she'll begin to discover even more deeply all the wonderful blessings God has given to each of you. Among those blessings: He led you to each other and gave you love and respect for your fiancée, and you're dedicated to walking through life by her side, serving and leading her to fully live as the woman God created her to become.

DAY 21

Model Your Leadership After Christ's

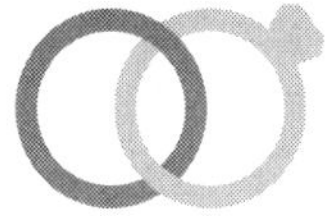

Early in our marriage, Mike and I stepped into a marriage bear trap that kept us chained to a place of hurt for a long time. I had started a late-night discussion during a post-pregnancy time of insecurity about my own attractiveness, worried I was losing his attention. In the context of what he naïvely thought was an innocuous conversation about what makes a woman attractive to a man, I asked him something along the lines of "Like what women?" He answered with several names. That argument swirled into anger and unkind words lasting into the wee hours of the night.

In that moment, we both let Jesus slip out of first place in our minds and hearts. Mike's justifying his answer and my refusal to believe he wasn't showing lack of love for me were just two symptoms that we had put ourselves above each other and each other above Jesus.

Putting ourselves above our spouses takes Jesus out of first place because He, our example, told us to turn the other cheek, to go the extra mile, to give more than is demanded. The One we're called to follow, even picking up our own crosses, washed the feet of His betrayer and prayed for the forgiveness of people as they crucified Him.

Had I kept Jesus first in that moment, I still would have cried. I still would have been hurt. I still could have been angry. But I wouldn't have stormed away as Mike had tried to apologize. I wouldn't have refused to listen to him explain. I wouldn't have lashed out in anger at the one I'm called to submit to as unto the Lord.

Had Mike kept Jesus in first place, he might have still given a dumb answer that deeply hurt me, but he wouldn't have blamed me for the misunderstanding. He wouldn't have gotten defensive and frustrated when I began to cry. He wouldn't have refused to give up a night's sleep for the one he's supposed to love as Christ loved His bride, laying down His very life for her.

The Alpha and Omega

Jesus is the beginning of all things, including offering insight into how to be a husband. As with every aspect of your life, you're called to follow Christ's model for your relationship. Keeping Him as your first love is the best step toward a lifelong marriage.

John 1:1-5 says of Jesus,

> In the beginning was the Word, and the Word was with God, and the Word was God. He was in the beginning with God. All things were made through him, and without him was not any thing made that was made. In him was life, and the life was the light of men. The light shines in the darkness, and the darkness has not overcome it.

Jesus stands as the source of all from the beginning. He is the Alpha and Omega. He belongs in first place, but it's easy to *say* He's there while really meaning He just has a place of importance in our minds. It's likely that Jesus does hold a place of importance in your mind. But being important doesn't mean He's in first place.

We know that the life of a person who proclaims Jesus as Lord should look different from the life of a person who doesn't. We also know that as we grow in our faith we should look more and more like Jesus. Sadly, we often fall short. Thankfully, His mercies are new every morning, so we continue to run the race.

Jesus has been important to Mike and me for most of our lives, but we had to make changes in our lives for Him to be put in first place. In fact, we must continually work to keep Him first.

Our commitment to that goal accounts for the fact that we're still married. For better, for worse, for richer, for poorer, in sickness, in health—we've walked through all those stages.

While we start with that commitment, keeping Jesus there is a day-to-day choice that requires us to honestly assess and reassess our priorities and to make changes when our priorities slip out of order. Our marriage attests to that fact.

A strong desire to follow Jesus started for me when I was eight years old. I still remember sitting on the front pew of our modest church one Sunday morning. I vividly recall looking down at my little black Mary Janes swinging back and forth as tears rolled down my cheeks and plopped onto my lap. I knew, even at eight, as I waited to be baptized, that I wanted and needed Jesus to be the Lord of my life.

Mike was baptized at age twenty-four, months after we met and years after beginning his search to figure out exactly what his faith entailed. He had grown up attending a Presbyterian congregation and had gone through a formal, intense study, a communicants' class, during junior high that had culminated in an interview with an elder and a public statement of faith.

Though we came from different denominations, we both believed in the authority of God, in the inspiration of Scripture, and that salvation is found only in Jesus. We both believed He should have first place in our hearts.

We made that initial declaration and commitment as a couple early in our marriage. However, we tended to view it a bit like our marriage vows—more a theoretical ideal or overarching concept than the driving force behind our day-to-day decisions and actions.

Time and Money

Two clear indicators of what holds first place in our lives are where we spend our time and where we spend our money. And of the two, time probably reveals more.

For the first three and a half years of our marriage, Mike and I had no children. We both worked, and that left about eighty waking hours per week. We viewed that time as ours to enjoy. Together, we spent time with his parents, double-dated with friends, played volleyball, went fishing, rode four-wheelers, and traveled. Mike worked out, played tennis, hung out with his buddies, and hunted. I read, shopped, worked out, and spent one weekend in my hometown in Texas with family and friends every month or so.

Almost every Sunday, we slept a bit later and struggled a bit more to get out of bed than on any other day. We attended worship services regularly, but almost every one of those Sunday mornings included one of us saying something like "It's getting late. Are we going?" We sometimes read our Bible. We prayed together when we ate together. Occasionally we prayed together at other times. We prayed some privately.

During those pre-kid years, we didn't earn a lot of money, but we had more than enough for the essentials and managed to go out for meals several times a month. We traveled a bit too. Most Sundays, we dropped a check into the offering plate after one of us nudged the other, who hurriedly filled out a check with an amount usually comparable to the cost of an average date night.

Contrast those norms with our church life today. Back then, we attended regularly, but more from obligation than true desire. Now we often arrive early enough to get to know people, help with some part of the setup, or pray. We look forward to worship, and we fully participate. We genuinely miss it when we can't attend. The sermons and lessons touch us in a personal way. We routinely pray—at meals, in the morning, at night, when we worry about someone or something, when we get good news, and when we get bad news. We read our Bible separately, and we read it aloud together. Waking hours focused on Jesus are double what they were early in our marriage.

Most important, our hearts have changed. There's no doubt about whether we're going to church or how much we're giving. Instead, we follow our commitments. Our online giving is automated so it happens even if we're not present. We agree on the amount we're able to give and review it at least once a year to be sure we're giving as we've committed.

Attending church and giving money don't prove faith or that Jesus reigns in our lives. Those two activities in our early years compared to today actually look similar from an external view, but the change in our hearts bears out the difference between when Jesus is just a part of our lives and when He holds first place.

Impact of the Fall

God built a deep longing into your very DNA for a relationship with Him. But since the fall, our sin has created a barrier. That first sin was a victorious initial foray of an enemy who wants to separate us from God, to tempt us into giving first place to anyone or anything other than God, to turn our hearts to idols. The father of lies tells you that you can give first place to yourself or to other people or activities—your wife, your future, your career, your children, sex, material wealth—and find fulfillment there. He's a liar bent on destroying.

When we give primacy to anyone or anything but God, we've created an idol. One of the biggest temptations will be to try to fill the deep longing for God with your marriage, to let your wife take first place. Don't allow your marriage or your wife to come before Jesus.

What It Looks Like

For Mike and me, our shared faith was a key part of our decision to date, get engaged, and marry. Throughout our marriage, we've worshiped together, attended Bible studies, and even taught Bible classes together. Yet for years I felt embarrassed, grieved, and a bit ashamed that, in spite of both of us being fully committed to Jesus, we've had a lot of brokenness and sin in our lives.

On this side of the halfway mark of my life, I've come to realize that having Jesus as Lord doesn't keep us from sinning or from brokenness. We all sin. Nor does keeping Jesus first mean you have an easy life. We all face hurt and heartache. Jesus died so that my brokenness and sin will be fully redeemed and my story, even with all its mess, can be used to help others.

So, practically speaking, what else does keeping Jesus first look like in your marriage?

Keeping Jesus first can be seen in how you fight, forgive, and reconnect. You *will* fight with each other. You're two flawed human beings committing to live together for life. What other commitment begins with no end date except death? With whom have you lived for even as short a time as a school semester without disagreements? Which one of your siblings did you not fight with when you lived together? This subject is so important that several chapters in this book will be devoted to the subject of how to fight well with your wife.

Keeping Jesus first also means that when you feel used by your spouse, you measure it against Jesus' plumb line: Go the extra mile. Love as He loves: "Greater love has no one than this, that someone lay down his life for his friends" (John 15:13). Keeping Jesus first means you forgive as He forgives you.

When you sin and when life is hard, return to the foot of the cross and lay your sins and your heartache down. Lay disappointment and hurt and even your marriage—when it's bad *and* when it's good—there as well, because that's where He paid for it all.

When we lay our lives at the foot of His cross, then Jesus, who is no longer on that cross but has risen from the grave and ascended to heaven, will redeem and restore our lives and all the scars for His glory and our good.

Live your lives so that everyone who comes to know you as husband and wife sees Jesus as the first and last in your life together. He is your first love. He is salvation and life and strength. The divine truth and irony of life is that the minute we allow anything to gain margin over our commitment to Christ, we will begin to lose whatever we have allowed to grow too important.

Let all who get to know you as a couple see that you have both kept Jesus as the Alpha and the Omega, the first and last, in your life together. Let people hear His invitation through you and your marriage: "Come! . . . Drink freely of the Water of Life!" (Revelation 22:17, MSG).

Countdown Journal

How will you keep Jesus as both the first and the last in your marriage?

How will your marriage invite others to meet Jesus?

Anniversary Reflection

After almost a year of marriage, what needs to change so that Jesus is first in your heart and in your marriage?

DAY 20

Seek the Kingdom of God First

Seeking the Kingdom of God first started early in Mike's and my dating relationship with a discussion about how important it was to me to only date someone who shared the commitment to do that. It was an uncomfortable conversation.

Mike was responsive to my stance on the matter, but our conversation wasn't easy. From the earliest days of our relationship, it was obvious that my place in the middle of seven children in a loud, opinionated family made me more comfortable with hard discussions than Mike. He had grown up as the only child of two of the most gentle, quiet people I've ever known. His willingness to keep having this tough conversation helped me believe he felt as attracted to me as I was to him.

When Jesus said, "Seek first the kingdom of God" (Matthew 6:33), He was tilting the worldview, launching the ministry that would turn the world upside down. The Sermon on the Mount challenges people to rethink who they are in relation to God, dig past their passive inaction down to their core motives, and realign their priorities. Jesus calls us to aggressively pursue God.

The calling is not to value God on the higher end of a list of favorite people and things. The calling is not to include the Kingdom in our cluster of places to go. The call is to *seek first the Kingdom of God.* Seeking is not a feeling, not a desire. Jesus calls us to an action, one that indicates that some difficulty will be encountered, aggressive effort will be required, focus will be needed, and distractions must be countered.

Seeking God first allows Him to fulfill all the other desires of your heart. In Matthew 6:33, Jesus says, "Seek first the kingdom of God . . . and all these things will be added to you."

This time of preparing to be married is the right time to start seeking the Kingdom first in your lives. You're taking many steps for ordering your lives together, laying the foundations for a lifelong partnership. You're making decisions about where you'll live, how you'll worship together, what you'll buy, how much you'll spend, and who will be your close friends. Some of those decisions are happening even when you're not devoting much time to deciding about them, but your actions reveal your choices. This is a time to prioritize intentional decisions. Don't fall into a pattern of passive choices, paths of least resistance.

> Value the power of intentionality.

How We Met

Mike and I met at a softball game in his hometown of Crossett, Arkansas. I was visiting from out of town for a job interview and only attended the game because a sweet young couple, Steven and Serena, had invited me. Knowing that my faith was central for me, the director of the hospital where I was interviewing had arranged for Steven and Serena to take me to a Bible study on Wednesday. Because I was staying overnight in Crossett after interviewing for the job, they invited me to the game and to go out for pizza.

After the game, Steven introduced me to Mike. Oblivious to the attempt to connect us, Mike turned down the offer to join us and left with another girl. I wasn't disappointed. Though Mike turned the heads of most girls, mine included, I had only interviewed for the job to get interviewing experience. I had already decided I was not taking the job, which paid too little and was probably a bit over my head as a new college graduate. Therefore, I had no interest in dating anyone in a town that was too small for a Burger King or a mall or a movie theater.

God had His plan, however. Less than a month later, I moved to Crossett with a one-year contract to work at the hospital as the director of public relations and personnel. Yes, the hospital was so small that they hired a brand-new graduate and gave me two jobs, HR and PR.

I had grown up with the crystal-clear voice of my mom in my head: "You won't marry everyone you date, but you won't marry anyone you don't date—so only date believers." I took that advice, though I had casually dated a lot of guys. In my mind, most dates weren't serious. In fact, many were only as "just friends."

The little church I began to attend in Crossett had four adult singles in the congregation. With a clear plan to be in Crossett for only one year, I wasn't concerned. I was moving back to Dallas soon and expected not to date in Crossett.

Mike had dated only a few women and really hadn't paid attention to their faith. He had dated to have girlfriends and have fun. But after completing college, he had begun to worry about that approach, and he had started to look for a serious relationship. He was worried he wouldn't find the kind of girl he wanted to marry in such a small town.

Did I mention that God had a plan?

During my first weeks living in Crossett, I saw Mike around town several times. After all, Crossett had fewer than fourteen thousand residents, so running into each other wasn't that surprising. One Sunday morning, however, Mike walked into the church I was attending with the same girl he had taken out after the ball game. Several weeks later, he and she quit dating, and he asked me out. That visit to the church had opened a door.

We were both believers, but we had grown up in different denominations and with different levels of exposure to Scripture. Worshiping together as a couple was a nonnegotiable for both of us, however. We knew decisions and changes would have to be made so we could serve together, but we made a commitment to put Jesus first and find a way to worship and work together or else not continue dating.

One of my fears as we sorted through our differences was that I would insert myself too much into what needed to be his journey of faith. Because of my comfort with tough discussions and voiced disagreements and Mike's family's tendency to avoid those, we both knew that this was a real risk. Mike decided to go through a Bible study on his own with one of his trusted friends. He was baptized weeks later, and we began attending worship together every Sunday and Bible class every Wednesday.

Despite the Strong Start . . .

Despite that strong spiritual start to our relationship, the sad truth is that over the years we've often failed to seek the Kingdom of God first. The sad truth you face as you read this is that you have failed (and will fail) to do it too. We don't know of any person who can say he or she is faithful in every way. We're all broken and we all sin. But we can't simply excuse all this as human frailty either. There's more to it than just not being able to be perfect.

Far too often, we simply fail to focus. We let ourselves become overwhelmed with distractions and cares of the world. We're too much like Martha, focusing on the distractions rather than on Jesus.

When Jesus confronted her, He said, "Martha, Martha, you are anxious and troubled about many things, but one thing is necessary" (Luke 10:41-42). Today, many of us are much worse than Martha. Our culture pursues a perpetual state of distraction and trouble about many things. The twenty-four-hour news cycle, social media, fidget toys, video games on our phones, noise, lights, commotion—all keep us from having downtime, from taking time to really ponder, be purposeful, and plan. This compulsion to be anxious and troubled about many things is being wielded as a powerful tool of the enemy with the sole aim of keeping us from sitting at Jesus' feet.

But. Only. One. Thing. Is. Necessary. Even though Mike and I have been Christians for most of our lives and married for more than thirty years, we feel as if we're just now really beginning to learn this, to really listen to this, to act this out in our lives. Only one thing is necessary.

It took us far too long to make sitting at Jesus' feet a priority. For the first twenty-five years of our marriage, we missed the blessing of starting our days together in prayer and Scripture. We've gained much blessing from getting up just a bit earlier so we can read the Bible together, sit quietly with the Word, and pray together. We've prayed at meals and bedtime, and those are important, but they're brief and part of the process of preparing to do something else. We waited far too long to set a time together to just sit at Jesus' feet—to seek the Kingdom first.

Make a commitment now, together, about seeking God and His righteousness first. Decide how you'll keep that as a priority in your marriage and every facet of your lives. If you make plans together and define what this will look like, you'll be uniquely positioned to help each other and to challenge each other when this priority starts to slip. You'll know your wife better than her friends do. She'll know you better than your friends do. You'll grow even closer.

Challenge each other to look honestly at how you're investing your time, your thoughts, and your money. What do you think about when you have a quiet moment? What do you commit time to every day? What do you make sure gets priority on your daily calendar? What would a stranger believe about your priorities if he saw only your calendar and your banking information? Are you considering God first as you make your plans?

Don't believe the lie that you can wait and talk about this *someday*. Don't let the feeling of not being close enough yet keep you from breaking through to a deeper level of intimacy that you'll gain by having this conversation. Don't put this off. Start now.

The two of you are right in the middle of huge distractions—engagement parties, wedding planning, dating, work. However, still, only one thing is necessary. Stop all the noise of this moment. Shut it out for a couple of minutes right now. Stop for just three minutes, 180 seconds. No noise, no commotion—just one focus: Seek first the Kingdom of God.

Set a timer for three minutes. Close your eyes, open your heart, hear Jesus call you to slam the door on the world's rush and rumble, and sit at His feet with Mary. (Seriously, set down this book, close your eyes, and meditate on Jesus' words "Seek first the kingdom of God" for three minutes. *Start the timer.*)

Right now, while you're especially distracted and troubled about many things, make a commitment to spend time seeking the Kingdom first—*starting today.*

When the buzzer goes off, jot down your meditations from this moment at Jesus' feet so you can share them with your fiancée. Carve out some time today to discuss your thoughts with her and start seeking first the Kingdom of God together. Maybe you'll decide to take Jesus' words literally, as Mike and I now do, and make shared prayer and Bible reading your first activity of the day.

Maybe early mornings won't work for you, but you can still make this your first priority by setting a time on your calendar that does work—even if it has to change from week to week or day to day. The key is to pursue God above all the distractions. Talk about how you'll do this together. It's the key to all the other things being added to your life.

Delight yourself in the Lord,
and he will give you the desires of your heart.

PSALM 37:4

Countdown Journal

What will you yourself do to seek first the Kingdom of God and His righteousness—daily, weekly, monthly, annually?

Anniversary Reflection

How have you lived up to your commitment from last year to seek the Kingdom of God first?

In your marriage, what do you want to do more of or less of so you can focus on Kingdom work together?

DAY 19

Keep Marriage in God's Perspective

When Mike and I announced our engagement, Mike's mom and dad offered us a piece of their land in Crossett. We bought a mobile home and parked it on the property, something I viewed as both budget friendly and temporary. We ended up living there for five years. The shared property was both a blessing and a curse; it actually tightened the apron strings rather than cutting them.

Mike continued to see his parents daily. We ate Sunday lunch at their home. During the workweek, Mike went home for lunch almost every day—*his mom's* home. It just made sense; his mom, Oneida, was retired, our house was next door, and she actually cooked lunch. I tended to have lunch meetings at the hospital. Then when I left the hospital to become a teacher, I was scheduled most days for lunch duty.

Looking back, we both now realize that those choices, while seeming to be natural, justifiable, and even wise, actually hinted at a brewing issue of not keeping God's perspective on marriage, which is to leave your father and mother and become one with your spouse. Did us living on their property and Mike having lunch at his parents' house save us money? Did it keep Mike tethered to them? Did it give more access and influence to his parents and challenge our oneness? Yes—to all.

Becoming One

God instituted marriage from the beginning to be an unbreakable connection: a man and a woman joined by God for life, becoming one flesh. In Genesis 2:24, God says, "A man shall leave his father and his mother and hold fast to his wife, and they shall become one flesh."

From God's perspective, this relationship stands out as markedly different from every other. You leave your parents, you decisively separate from Mom and Dad, and you become one flesh with your wife.

Mike and I knew this Scripture. The preacher quoted it at our wedding. Like most people, we glossed over the real meaning and romanticized it. We didn't really understand it, and we certainly didn't embody it. In fact, our connections to our parents created early struggles. Both of us loved and respected our parents and were blessed to have parents who had raised us to believe in God. We also both had parents who tended to be a bit controlling, although in very different manners.

I felt loud and a bit intrusive from the moment I walked into Mike's parents' home to meet them. Even as I tried to lean all my weight on my toes, my wooden wedge heels clunked across the hardwood floors of the quietest home I had ever entered. Within that peaceful home lived two of the most soft-spoken and kind people I'd ever met.

Over the first years of our marriage, I found the quiet of Mike's childhood home a bit unsettling and tried to speak softer and less often. I quickly discovered that topics such as the weather, daily activities, sports, hunting, and food were preferred. Topics such as future plans, especially any that might include a job change or a move away from Mike's hometown, took the quiet to a deafening level.

Differences and Conflict

The first time I took Mike home to Texas, eight rowdy nieces and nephews met us at the door of our car, the noise of my big family rolling out of my parents' home. Mike inadvertently, but quite literally, positioned himself in the farthest corner from the centers of activity, the kitchen and dining area. He would engage in the games and conversations, but the whole experience seemed to exhaust him. The debates and arguments that erupted from time to time shocked him.

Mike struggled with the always-direct, often-loud, and many-times-confrontational style of my parents. To be honest, so did I. In fact, the idea of getting some distance from that style had played a role in my choice to attend a college more than seven hours from home.

From the day we met, Mike knew I had a definitive plan to move back to Texas or, at the very least, stay in Arkansas but move to Little Rock or Searcy—to a place with a strong church and better job opportunities, museums, and theaters. We both had jobs in Crossett, but we were both interviewing elsewhere.

However, our tendency to revert to the communication styles of our childhoods and to assign expectations to our marriage based on our families of origin set up long-term negative patterns. My deep desire for us to leave Mike's hometown and the unchanged connection between Mike and his parents fueled many of our arguments. The vast difference in our approaches to those disagreements created even bigger issues.

Not only did Mike and I miss the point of God's first edict on marriage—to leave the child role and all its dependency on parents—but our parents did as well. Mike's mom voiced her disapproval of his looking for a job anywhere else by seeding doubt and fear of change and being "so worried for him" that she had to stay in bed at times. Mine teased and wheedled me about being the only child who'd moved away. And when I called to tell Mom we were engaged, she voiced her disappointment that she "just knew you would do this and marry someone out of state."

We weren't the first to struggle to do marriage God's way. Barely out of the garden of Eden, mankind tossed God's perspective on marriage. People quickly embraced divorce, allowed by Moses, and walked away from marriage for just about any reason. More than once in Jesus' ministry, He challenged this misuse of the law on divorce. In His full authority, He emphasized the permanency of marriage. "He said to them, 'Because of your hardness of heart Moses allowed you to divorce your wives, but from the beginning it was not so. And I say to you: whoever divorces his wife, except for sexual immorality, and marries another, commits adultery'" (Matthew 19:8-9).

Jesus' declaration stunned the disciples. They found it unreasonable: "If such is the case of a man with his wife," they said, "it is better not to marry" (Matthew 19:10).

Jesus didn't disagree: "Not everyone can receive this saying, but only those to whom it is given" (Matthew 19:11).

Look carefully at what Jesus said next to those who found His stance on marriage too hard. He suggested becoming a eunuch—that is, medically celibate. Don't miss the impact, the shocking difficulty, of what Jesus told His followers: "There are eunuchs who have been so from birth, and there are eunuchs who have been made eunuchs by men, and there are eunuchs who have made themselves eunuchs for the sake of the kingdom of heaven. Let the one who is able to receive this receive it" (Matthew 19:12).

Jesus makes it clear that marriage is a lifelong commitment, and if you think that's too hard—if you aren't committed until death—don't go through with it.

How's that for setting the bar high? Marriage until death or don't get married. This is a God-ordained union, so stay celibate or stay married—that's God's perspective.

It's Not Easy

The same Bible that presents God's perspective on marriage shows just how hard it can be. Scripture tells the stories of many marriages, and nearly every one involves sin, heartache, brokenness, and loss. A few that come immediately to mind include the unions of Adam and Eve, Abraham and Sarah, Hosea and Gomer, David and Michal, David and Bathsheba, and Solomon and some seven hundred wives and three hundred concubines.

Adam and Eve started with the perfect marriage, literally walking with God in a beautiful garden. Because of sin, they (and every couple since) faced shame, having to work under stress and struggle, and pain in childbirth. They were evicted from their home. They suffered the death of a child. They faced a lifetime of separation from Cain because of his sentence for murdering his brother.

Abraham left Sarah exposed two different times as a sex object for other men in order protect himself. Sarah and Abraham tried unsuccessfully for decades to have a child. Because they didn't trust God to fulfill His promise, they contrived a sordid plan to make Abraham a father. He forced an enslaved woman, Hagar, to bear him a son. When Sarah's jealousy flared up, he and Sarah abandoned Hagar and Ishmael, Hagar's child with Abraham.

David and Michal were torn apart by in-law conflict and power struggles. Their disagreement over how to worship led to Michal expressing contempt toward David, and that resulted in her inability to have a child. Her own father forced her to marry another man while she was still married to David. David also had at least five other marriages, some of which we know were full of heartbreak. Perhaps the worst example is the relationship of David and Bathsheba. Their relationship began with adultery, and then David orchestrated her husband's murder. Their firstborn child died as an infant. They, too, lost God's perspective on marriage.

Solomon wrote the Song of Solomon for one very loved unnamed bride. This book of erotic and romantic love poetry provides not only an allegory of the deep love of God for His people, of Jesus for the church, but also insight into God's will for a man and woman to be together naked and unashamed (see Genesis 2:25). But Solomon married some seven hundred women and eventually turned away from God because of his wives who worshiped other gods. Despite authoring portions of the Old Testament and being gifted by God with great intellect and insight, Solomon completely lost God's perspective on marriage.

Throughout the Bible, in all history, among acquaintances, and even up close in our families, we see indisputable proof of the difficulty of marriage. The divorce rate today is alarmingly high and goes even higher for marriages beyond the first.

Yet even though we're surrounded by scriptural, statistical, and anecdotal evidence of the difficulty of marriage, most every one of us, including Mike and me, walks into marriage expecting it to be filled with joy and laughter, fulfilled expectations, and few, if any, arguments.

We all know marriage isn't easy, and we understand and really mean the commitment our vows promise. But then, just a few months (or days) down the road, someone complains about how much time the other spends working out or one spends too much money on coffee. Somebody is messy. A snide comment leads to a big fight. Cross words turn into indictments of character. Hurt feelings quickly become false evidence of a lack of love. If that pattern continues for any period, love wanes.

"For richer or poorer," we proclaim, but then we argue when they spend a hundred dollars from our savings account on a new pair of shoes. "In sickness and in health," we promise, but one of us sulks in the living room when the other doesn't feel well enough to go out with friends. We promise to forsake all others and then put more effort into helping a friend than helping each other. We say, "I'll love you more than anyone." Yet, as years slip by, we find it harder to be as gentle with our spouse as we are with our coworkers. We say, "I'll do anything for you." Then we lose our temper over having to shut cabinet doors left open or being reminded about the chore we promised to do two weeks ago but still haven't.

The statistics about and the reality of failed marriages are discouraging, but don't let the enemy convince you that marriage is impossible. *With God, all things are possible!* Every intact marriage requires work and sacrifice; a good marriage requires great work, deep sacrifice, flowing forgiveness, and a commitment to keep Jesus at the center. You can't do it by yourself, and you can't do it by letting the marriage take on more importance than God.

Your relationship with God can even pave the way to restoring your marriage if it seems to have reached the point of no return. When a marriage is falling apart, God can save it. Thankfully, through Him, impossible situations become possible.

Keeping God's Perspective

Your wedding, your love, your marriage—they matter to God, to your extended families, to your future. Your marriage and your love for each other are part of God's plan for your lives. But don't let the lies of this world and the enemy deceive you: Your wedding, your love, and your marriage must pale in comparison to your commitment to follow Jesus, to be like Jesus, to keep Him your first love.

In all history, no wife has ever been perfect. In all history, only one man has ever been perfect—and you aren't Him.

Just as your love for each other must pale in comparison to your love for Jesus, God's first guideline for marriage is that your relationship with your parents—or, for that matter, anyone you have relied on or who has relied on you—must also pale in comparison to your relationship with your wife. Leave father and mother. Leave and cleave. You two are to become one flesh and forsake all others.

Christ's commitment to His bride, the church, caused Him to leave His earthly mother to minister to broken and hurting people. His love for His bride caused Him not only to live sacrificially but also to die in her place.

Only by the indwelling of the Holy Spirit will you be able to truly desire to live as a Christ-reflecting husband. So spend the next few weeks considering what that looks like as we count down to the second-most-important day of your life.

Countdown Journal

How will you keep marriage in perspective—to leave parents, forsake all others, and become one flesh with your future wife?

What patterns have been established by or with your parents or others on whom you rely that need to be broken so you can become one flesh with your wife and build a healthy marriage?

Anniversary Reflection

How well have you kept marriage in perspective—leaving Mom and Dad, forsaking others, and becoming one flesh with your wife?

Are there any patterns with your parents or friends that weaken your commitment to your marriage?

Which of your buddies are truly helping you live as a self-sacrificing servant-leader in a world that glorifies arrogance and misogyny? Do any of your friends make it harder for you to honor your marriage? In what ways?

DAY 18

Embrace the Unity of the Holy Spirit

Mike and I both were raised in religious environments that tended to stifle any discussion of, let alone evidence of the working of, the Holy Spirit. In fact, any outward expression of anything except a somber and pious attitude was tamped down, squelched, quenched. Yet we read in 1 Thessalonians 5:19, "Do not quench the Spirit."

Then, early in our marriage, I attended a women's conference where God began to confront my heart with this verse and others. Thousands of women filled the stadium in Dallas, praising God and listening to preaching and teaching about Jesus. I can't remember a single speaker's name or the points of any of their lessons, but I can still vividly recall what God opened in my heart. From my seat way up in the balcony, as I sang along with Point of Grace, a movement down by the right side of the stage caught my eye.

Even from that distance, I could clearly see a young woman getting caught up in the worship song. She stretched her arms overhead and swayed. Then she stepped slowly out from her front row seat into the aisle, rising to the toes of her left foot and beginning a series of ballet moves.

What an attention hound, I thought, perched on the balcony where I edged from my very reserved worship right into judgmentalism. My attention turned fully toward her, realizing she even wore a leotard and tutu—a leotard and tutu! Then as I continued to watch her dance, a Bible story from 2 Samuel sprang into my mind.

David was leading the people of Israel as they returned the Ark of the Covenant to Jerusalem. The Bible describes his worship: "David *danced before the LORD with all his might*. . . . As the ark of the LORD came into the city of David, Michal the daughter of Saul looked out of the window and saw King David *leaping and dancing before the LORD*, and she despised him in her heart" (2 Samuel 6:14, 16, emphasis added).

I knew the story well enough that I immediately recognized myself and began to cry, fully indicted by David's response to Michal, who had accused him of drawing attention to himself, saying he was honoring himself with his vulgar dance and attire. David told her, "It was before the LORD, who chose me above your father and above all his house, to appoint me as prince over Israel, the people of the LORD—and I will celebrate before the LORD" (2 Samuel 6:21).

The story ends just two verses later with God's judgment: "Michal the daughter of Saul had no child to the day of her death" (2 Samuel 6:23).

That day began a journey of prying loose my grip on my own comfort level, my own preferences, and my self-proclaimed certainty of what is and is not authentic, Spirit-led worship. God confirmed that I needed to take that journey just a few weeks later as we hosted a group in our home to watch the Super Bowl. Sitting in my living room, waiting for the next incredible commercial and the upcoming halftime show (the only parts I really enjoyed), I studied the people in the room. Some leaned forward intently, silently watching as the next play unfolded. Some stood and paced as much as our small living room would allow.

When the pass sailing through the air dropped into the waiting arms of the wide receiver, the group erupted. Some danced, some shouted, some embraced. The only ones with a reserved response were those of us who really didn't care. But all those responses were perfectly fine, as are different forms of worship.

The Spirit's Role

The Holy Spirit, according to Scripture, affects every part of our lives! He can provide you with all you need to thrive in life and in marriage. As I worked on writing this chapter, Mike and I realized that we need to spend more time focusing on each of the ways the Holy Spirit acts in our lives and discovering more about how He leads and empowers us. You probably do too.

The Bible tells us that the Spirit

- guides us to truth, revealing the deep things of God (John 16:13; Romans 9:1; 1 Corinthians 2:10-11);
- gives us access to God the Father and helps us pray (Galatians 4:6; Ephesians 2:18);
- reveals the love and mystery of God to us (Romans 5:5; Ephesians 3:4-5);
- testifies of Christ and reveals Him to us (John 15:26; 16:14; 1 John 4:2);
- regenerates us, seals us for redemption, and guarantees our resurrection (John 3:5-8; 2 Corinthians 1:21-22; 5:5; Ephesians 1:13; 4:30; Titus 3:4-7);
- leads us, teaches us, and reminds us of the Word (Matthew 4:1; Luke 4:1; John 14:26; Romans 8:14; 1 Corinthians 2:13; Galatians 5:18);
- sanctifies us and frees us from the law of sin and death (Romans 5:5, 16; 8:2; 2 Thessalonians 2:13; 1 Peter 1:2);
- indwells and fills us (John 14:16-17; Acts 2:4; 4:8, 31; 9:17; Romans 8:9; Ephesians 5:18);
- produces fruit in and through us (Galatians 5:22-23);

- speaks to, in, and through us (Matthew 10:20; Acts 2:4; 8:29; 10:19; 11:12, 28; 13:2; 16:6-7; 21:4, 11; 1 Corinthians 12:3; 1 Timothy 4:1; Hebrews 3:7-11; Revelation 2:11);
- anoints us for ministry (Luke 4:18; Acts 13:2; 20:28; 2 Peter 1:21);
- comforts us, moves us, and gives us joy (Acts 9:31; 1 Thessalonians 1:6; 2 Peter 1:21);
- empowers healing, miracles, discernment, tongues, and artistry (Luke 24:49; Acts 1:8; Romans 15:19; 1 Corinthians 12:4, 8-10; Hebrews 2:4); and
- brings unity and oneness to the body (Ephesians 2:14-18; 4:1-3).

Convincing evidence of the Holy Spirit in a relationship is love and unity. Convincing evidence of His absence is anger and division.

The list above and the related Scriptures are a great starting place. Take a moment to review them. Pay attention to how the Holy Spirit empowers us to change our lives, especially our relationships. The Holy Spirit plays the same role in marriage that He does in the Godhead and the church. He brings unity and oneness.

Note also this promise from Jesus:

> "I tell you, ask, and it will be given to you; seek, and you will find; knock, and it will be opened to you. For everyone who asks receives, and the one who seeks finds, and to the one who knocks it will be opened. . . . If you then, who are evil, know how to give good gifts to your children, *how much more will the heavenly Father give the Holy Spirit to those who ask him!*"
>
> LUKE 11:9-10, 13, EMPHASIS ADDED

As parents, we want to give our children wonderfully good gifts. We often stretch or strain our financial limits to do so. If it's in our power to give something to our children that will make their lives better, we make it happen. But according to this overwhelming promise of Jesus, God is much more willing and able to do this. Jesus repeats this promise of God's responsiveness three times—ask and receive, seek and find, knock and enter. Then He doubles down on the promise—everyone who asks receives, whoever seeks finds, and whoever knocks enters.

Verse 13 takes it even further. The good gift God offers, better than any gifts given by human parents, is the gift of the Holy Spirit.

Only the Holy Spirit can adequately empower you to become the man God intends you to be, in life and in your marriage. As you ask for Him, He indwells and empowers you at the level you let Him reign. The Holy Spirit reveals the love of God, frees us from the bondage of the law, sanctifies us, indwells and empowers us, comforts us, unifies us, and produces the fruit of love, joy, peace, patience, kindness, goodness, faithfulness, gentleness, and self-control.

Regarding the Spirit's role in creating unity: Not only will you and your wife become one flesh because of the physical union of sex, but you will also be made one by the indwelling Holy Spirit. In Philippians 2, Paul says, "If there is any encouragement in Christ, any comfort from love, any participation in the Spirit, any affection and sympathy, complete my joy by being of the same mind, having the same love, being in full accord and of one mind" (Philippians 2:1-2).

When God unites a man and woman in marriage, two become one: Two people indwelled by the Holy Spirit become one flesh.

Paul wrote this to all believers. How much more does it apply to the two believers forged into one flesh in marriage by God?

A few years ago, Mike touched my heart in the most powerful way during a prayer. At the end of the prayer, he said, "We ask this not as two separate people but as one body, joined together, sanctified in marriage by You." He had never said that before. I'm not sure what prompted it. But he now ends almost every one of our private prayers that way. I can't tell you how much it touches a very deep place in my heart. Every time.

Opposing the Spirit

The Holy Spirit is God's gift to us. But like all God's gifts, we can accept it or reject it. Scripture warns against three specific ways we might oppose the Spirit. We can grieve the Spirit. We can try to usurp the role of the Spirit. And we can quench the Spirit.

Right in the middle of a series of warnings against lying, stealing, corrupting talk, bitterness, wrath, anger, evil speech, and malice, Paul warns, "Do not grieve the Holy Spirit of God, by whom you were sealed for the day of redemption" (Ephesians 4:30). Those sins against another person actually grieve the Spirit, the One who unifies people in love. Instead, Paul says, we should "be kind to one another, tenderhearted, forgiving one another, as God in Christ forgave you" (Ephesians 4:32).

You can only be empowered to be a man of God, to intentionally model Christ as the true Bridegroom, through the power of the Holy Spirit. You are indwelled by His power.

Your fiancée is also indwelled by the Spirit, and He knows both your hearts. In under three weeks, God will unite you with her in marriage, making you one flesh. A powerful bond is created between a man and a woman who are sexually intimate. That bond is also supernatural and miraculous because God has joined it together. The Holy Spirit unites each of you with Jesus, and He indwells you in your oneness as a husband and wife.

You don't have all the answers. You can't control others or change their destiny. You're not the arbiter of right and wrong. Neither is your wife. Neither am I, nor is my husband. But I've been known to try with Mike and Mike with me, and we've seen many of our friends do the same with their spouses.

Not only can we grieve the Holy Spirit or try to put ourselves in His position, but we can also quench the Spirit and minimize His impact. First Thessalonians 5:19 says directly and simply, "Do not quench the Spirit." To quench something is to extinguish, subdue, quell, or destroy it. If we quench the Spirit, we're damaging unity, subduing love, quelling the teaching and guidance we need, and destroying God's fruit in our lives.

For much of my life, I've tended to ignore that passage or read it as a warning not to disregard or not to grieve the Spirit. We're capable of both those errors and warned against them, but the Greek word here rendered *quench* is unique, and it doesn't mean "ignore" or "grieve." The word means "stifle" or "suppress" and almost always has to do with fire in the Bible. Interestingly, the Holy Spirit appeared as tongues of fire at Pentecost.

We can grieve Him by sinning against one another, or we can let Him lead us in kindness, tenderheartedness, and forgiveness. We can try to usurp His place, or we can grow in His unity by letting Him guide us and sanctify us to be more and more like Jesus. We can quench the Spirit, or we can ask for more of Him—growing in His might and unity.

Spend time with your wife focusing on the Holy Spirit's role in your lives and your marriage. And be patient with each other as the Holy Spirit works in you individually and as one flesh.

Countdown Journal

What will be evidence that you're relying on the Holy Spirit in your life and marriage?

How do you tend to quench the Spirit? How will you change that?

Anniversary Reflection

What fruit has your marriage produced that is evidence of the Holy Spirit?

How can you grow more fruit in and through your marriage?

DAY 17

Fight for Her, Not with Her

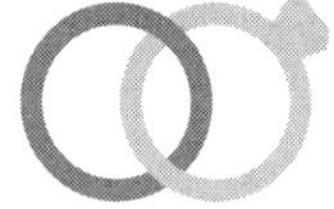

Mike and I had our first real fight two years into our marriage. On a crisp November weekend, he had plans to hunt on a Saturday, but I was feeling terribly ill that Friday night as we went to bed. He less-than-enthusiastically offered to stay home.

I didn't want him to go, but I also didn't want him to miss hunting. I knew he'd be disappointed, and neither of us handled disappointment well. I also knew I was really getting sick—sore throat, cough, and achy joints. I'm pretty independent but couldn't imagine being home alone all day with what threatened to be the flu.

I hesitantly suggested maybe he could go in the morning but please not leave me alone all day. I hoped he would flatly cancel. He agreed he could tell the guys he was cutting the day short and promised he would be home well before lunch. And, of course, he said he would tell his mom to check on me. I demurred.

He did come home well before lunch. I was relieved. I needed NyQuil, throat lozenges, Popsicles, soup, and hot tea. We had none of those. I asked him to run to the store. He said he was "pretty sure Mom has some stuff we could use." He went to his mom's next door. When he got back, he helped me move to the couch and gave me some ibuprofen and off-brand cough medicine from his mom's. There were no Popsicles. He had brought back peppermints but no throat lozenges. With a bit of guidance, he managed to make me some lunch. He sat on the couch beside me, and we both fell asleep.

I woke to the distinctive, obnoxious sound of his hunting buddy's truck roaring into our driveway. Mike was sheepishly glancing over at me as he eased the back door open and started to slip outside. He realized I was awake at about the same time I realized he was leaving.

"Hey," he said, stepping back inside. "I was thinking you might be asleep for a while."

"Did you not tell him you were staying home this afternoon?" I croaked, my brows so deeply furrowed there could be no doubt how I felt.

He said something about wanting to wait to see if I felt better before he disappointed the guys.

"Of course," I muttered. "Go on. I can take care of myself."

He hesitated. Then he went out the door.

I went to the bathroom, and when I came out, the truck noises were long gone. I put a tea bag in a cup, added water, set out a lemon on the cutting board, and opened the drawer to get a knife. I slammed the drawer, and it felt so good that I slammed it again. In the process, I bumped the cutting board, which knocked the cup over, spilling water everywhere. That made me so mad that I threw the knife as hard as I could into the sink and followed it in quick succession with the cutting board and the cup, which shattered.

That kind of noise in a mobile home is loud—loud enough that it echoed outside, where my husband and his hunting buddy were sitting on the tailgate of the truck he had turned off while I'd been in the bathroom.

The fight that followed was full of denial and blame. We did not resolve our conflict even though Mike stayed home.

If it were to get to that point today, I would laugh when he opened the back door and slowly peeked in to see what had happened instead of snapping "Get out!" because of my own embarrassment. When he said, "What in the world did you do?" I would detail the ridiculous series of unfortunate events, sharing every silly moment until he was laughing with me. When he said, "What's wrong with you?" I would say, "I want us to be a strong team, and when I'm feeling sick or down, I need you, just you, to be with me."

But that argument was a full-on fight for us. Maybe the truer way to describe it would be as a full-on fight *against* each other. He was wrong. I was out of control. He was abandoning me. I was being ridiculous. Me against him. Him against me.

Honestly, if it were today, the fight would have begun on Friday evening so I could have fought *for* him instead of *against* him. I should have been direct in saying, "I need you to stay home tomorrow. I need *you*; please don't pull your mom into this. And it will mean a lot to me if you make the extra effort to go get what I really want at the store."

When he obviously wanted to go hunting anyway, now I would say, "I know you want to go, and I get it, but I need you here." If he chose to go anyway, I would go ahead and cry, not hiding a bit of the hurt from him, go to bed, and pray myself to sleep.

You *Will* Fight

A day is coming—and coming soon (if it hasn't already happened)—when one or both of you will lose your temper like never before. You may find yourself saying and doing some of the most hurtful things you have ever said or done to another person. My prayer is that you'll be better than we've been, more prepared to battle *for* each other rather than *with* each other. We have a powerful enemy who thrives on misdirecting our fights against each other rather than against him.

Scripture is honest about this horrible broken pattern in marriage. From Adam to Abraham to David and every generation between and since, sin has devastated marriages and families. We show the worst disregard for and commit the most hurtful acts against those who are the closest to us, most often the person we have chosen as our partner for life.

Start preparing for that battle now. Redirecting the battle at the true enemy is critical in breaking the strongholds Satan is already building against your marriage. "For we do not wrestle against flesh and blood, but against the rulers, against the authorities, against the cosmic powers over this present darkness, against the spiritual forces of evil in the heavenly places" (Ephesians 6:12).

This is so important and so hard that we're going to spend several days in this book covering how to fight well.

Mike and I wish we could go back to the early days of our marriage and formally, even perhaps in our wedding vows, commit to fighting well. The Bible is filled with stories of volatile confrontations, replete with advice on handling disagreements, laser focused on the identification of the source of arguments, and crystal clear that we're in a battle with supernatural forces at war in our physical world, hearts, and minds.

Yet we Christians are inclined to believe a dangerous delusion! We believe that we can expect endless harmony with one another, that conflict ought to happen rarely and be resolved quickly when it arises. We believe that if we really love each other we won't have big fights. Oh, sure, if we're pressed, we tsk-tsk and say, "Of course there will be disagreements; that's normal. We aren't naïve."

Know this: You will disagree. You will argue. You will fight. Learn to do it well.

The truth is, however, that deep at the core of what's wrong with how we disagree, argue, and fight is the fact that we believe that we shouldn't but that if we do it's a sign that the other person or the relationship itself is the wrong one.

Learn to enjoy and even celebrate disagreements. Embrace them as something that brings more diversity to your life. She'll want to dine out; you'll want to order in. She'll want to paint the room the palest of blues. You'll want white. She'll define clean as one level; you may not even see the difference in levels.

When a disagreement can't be worked with or around, then go ahead and argue. But make up your mind to argue in a way that honors Jesus. Don't let an argument end in a lose-lose. Don't let any argument end in a win-lose. And don't sweep arguments under the rug.

Not every disagreement has to be an argument. Not every little issue must be addressed. Forgiveness can, and sometimes should, be extended without the recipient even knowing. However, if the situation involves unrepented or ongoing sin, you must address it. If the situation is hurting you or causing you to withdraw or hide some part of yourself, it must be addressed. If the issue wounds, if anger is simmering, if one is hurt, then the argument needs to be faced. That's not optional; it's a biblical imperative and requires you to act.

The Biblical Imperative

That imperative lies in two passages from Matthew:

- If she has something against you, go to her and work it out; be reconciled (Matthew 5:23-24).
- If she has sinned, go to her and work it out; be reconciled (Matthew 18:15-17).

If you're fighting with your wife to exert your own good, your way, or your will, you aren't fighting well. If the issue is about her good or betterment and to honor God, you're obligated to put on the armor of God and take a stand (see Ephesians 6:10-18).

It took a long time, much too long and far too many wounds, for Mike and me to even begin to hear these commands with open and tender hearts. Instead, for some time, the verses seemed confusing because of a desire in my unforgiving heart to assign responsibility to someone else. *Surely if he has wronged me he's supposed to do the reconciling*, the corrupted heart reasons.

The legalistic heart argues for a just sentencing of the guilty party. And in our sinful hearts, we believe that if someone has wronged us, the person committing the wrong (and it's always the other person) should start the reconciliation.

But in both passages, Jesus assigns responsibility to the one hearing His words. We can't justify our inaction by another person's inaction. We can't justify nursing our wounds because it's "not my fault."

The person who loves Jesus, whether we've been sinned against or we've wounded another, is the one who must start the reconciliation process. The reality is that we were guilty but Jesus bought our redemption and forgave us while we were yet sinners. He set the perfect example.

> In our self-righteousness, we want the responsibility to be based on the guilt of the person, and we also want to be the judge who decides the guilt.

Scripture also reveals a predisposition we need to develop that's diametrically opposed to our natural bias. Rather than seeking to make someone else do something for us or waiting for that person to make the first move, our attitude should be that we will eagerly take the first steps to repair a relationship.

By nature, we resist admitting our most egregious behavior when the evidence can't be denied, but Jesus puts responsibility squarely on whoever follows Him to pursue reconciliation even when a person just has "something against us."

Having something against a person is a broad and ambiguous statement. The implication is that we must give weight to the other person's feelings and perceptions, that the burden of proving fault is not necessary when we're aware that a "brother has something against" us. Just knowing that is all we need to prompt us to go and seek reconciliation.

On the flip side, when we're considering whether we need to seek reconciliation because we've been aggrieved, Jesus says, "if your brother sins against you, go and tell him his fault, between you and him alone" (Matthew 18:15). I'm not saying you can't talk to another person if your feelings have been hurt, but Scripture certainly doesn't command it. The requirement for going to someone about how he or she has treated us is the higher bar—sin and fault: "If your brother sins against you, go and tell him his fault." The bar for going to someone about our own behavior is much lower—if a person *has something against you.*

This should not be twisted to obligate us to seek reconciliation when someone continues to hold something against us, but that's rarely our struggle. Our day-to-day struggle is to be humble enough to initiate reconciliation when we have completely wronged another person and we know it.

In Marriage

How you argue is critically important in your marriage. Don't ignore it. Don't just let the moment pass. Seek opportunities to learn about your wife's needs, to find out how you can honor her, to discover how to make big and small changes to keep from wounding her. When you sense she's feeling something against you, take the initiative, humble yourself, go to her, and work to make it better.

> The responsibility for initiating reconciliation is mine every time because Jesus pursued reconciliation with me through His death even while I was still sinning.

How can you know if you're fighting with her or for her? The key is the impact and the outcome you're seeking. If I could revisit our earliest days of marriage, I would change my approach to disagreements in many ways. We would fight, maybe quite a bit more often than we did in the beginning, but we would fight differently.

You and I are the ones commanded to seek reconciliation every time. We don't get to wait for the one we believe to be in the wrong to do the work. Speak this truth to yourself until your head and heart agree.

Countdown Journal

How will you keep your focus on fighting for your wife, not with her?

What will be warning signs that you're fighting the wrong fight?

Anniversary Reflection

How safe have you made your wife feel in sharing her opinions with you?

What can you do to encourage each other to focus on fighting the right fights for one another and not against one another?

DAY 16

Continue Steadfastly in Prayer

Mike and I didn't start out praying together regularly other than at meals. We had both grown up in families that had prayed before each meal, and that translated easily into our married life. I prayed on my own, and Mike did the same. I vividly remember the first time we prayed fervently together—more than four years into our marriage.

When our first son, Patrick, turned a month old, he became ill one Sunday afternoon, spitting up so much and so suddenly that we called the pediatrician, who told us to meet him at the emergency room. We honestly thought that at the ER we would be reassured he was fine and maybe come home with some medicine for a stomach virus.

At the ER, however, spitting up became projectile vomiting, and crying turned to wailing and then abruptly stopped. Patrick had quickly dehydrated. The medical team was trying unsuccessfully to draw blood and hook up fluids intravenously. Soon, more-skilled staff were called in, and then Patrick was rushed away from us. We knew we weren't going home anytime soon. Concern exploded into deep fear. We sat in the lobby and prayed together earnestly.

When Patrick had been in the hospital for almost a week, after test after test, IV antibiotics and fluids, and blown vein after blown vein, we believed the unidentified bacterial infection had been beaten. Patrick had finally been able to nurse without spitting up. He had regained some of the weight he had lost, and the deep, dark circles under his eyes had faded. We were to be discharged the next day. Mike and I had prayed more together in that week than in the previous four years combined.

As I changed Patrick's diaper on the hospital bed that afternoon, I watched a wave literally roll under his skin from the left to the right side of his tiny belly. Then he vomited violently. My mom called the nurse. The nurse called the doctor. I held Patrick as he cried.

Our pediatrician, Dr. Smith, came to the hospital and arrived at about the same time as Mike after he rushed back to the hospital from work. I tried to describe what I'd seen. Dr. Smith, who was examining Patrick, turned his attention fully to me and asked me to repeat myself. He told us he believed that Patrick was developing pyloric stenosis and would require surgery.

After days of not being able to nurse and several challenging situations involving unclear tests and medical-staff disagreements, Dr. Smith's suspicions were confirmed, and they let us carry our tiny, six-week-old baby to the doors of the operating room, where the surgeon himself took him from my arms.

While our family waited nearby, Mike and I went to the chapel. No longer just a shared mealtime activity, prayer together had become a powerful source of comfort and reassurance and our first line of defense and offense. We knelt and prayed together.

Patrick was nursing within two hours of that surgery. We were home and mostly back to normal in under forty-eight hours.

In Your Marriage

You already have full access to the ultimate defense against evil, the greatest tool for success, the wisest investment of time, and the key to strengthening your marriage—prayer. Before you turn to a friend, a book, a counselor, your parents, or a pastor, turn to God first. Paul tells us to "continue steadfastly in prayer" (Colossians 4:2).

When you're showered with blessings, when you can't see a way through, when difficulties overwhelm you, when joy fills your day, when little annoyances drive you nuts—pray. In Ephesians 6:18, Paul instructs us to be "praying at all times in the Spirit, with all prayer and supplication." Another translation renders this "pray in the Spirit on all occasions with all kinds of prayers and requests" (NIV).

In prayer, we communicate directly with the creator of the universe, the source of life and blessing. We have only to call out to Him, and He inclines His ear to us. He truly wants to hear our prayers. He invites us into His presence and promises to hear our petitions and answer us.

Pray for your wife. Your Father created her. He shaped her body, formed her face, painted her eyes, sculpted her lips. He breathed life into her lungs, tuned her voice, molded her mind, crafted her emotions, and filled her heart with the passion and desires He chose. He gave her the talents that will fulfill His plan. He knows her more intimately than you can and knows how to help you love her well.

Pray *with* your wife daily. Start now if you haven't already. Get up early enough to help her get her day started, to ensure that she has time to pray and spend time with God. Pray with her every night. Every. Night. Don't let your nighttime prayer get lost in fatigue or different bedtimes. Plan to pray before you're sleepy, and honor that commitment every night. Intentionally rework your schedules to be sure you spend meaningful time praying together. When you're in separate places, pray by phone.

When she cries, wrap your arms around her and pray over her. When she's ill, pray for her healing. When she's asleep and you're overwhelmed by her beauty, thank God for her. When she's away, pray for her protection. When she's grumpy, be sympathetic and say a silent prayer. When you're upset with her, pray for the Holy Spirit to speak to her heart on your behalf. When *she's* upset, pray for her to feel the presence and power of the Spirit.

Just as we learn about friends as we communicate with them, so also we learn about God as we communicate with Him. He reveals Himself by how He comforts us, giving us peace that surpasses understanding. He discloses Himself as He answers our prayers. God's character is also made known by the reasons He won't honor our prayers—unconfessed sin, selfish motives, or a lack of forgiveness.

> Your prayers for your wife will do more good than any words you can speak, any advice you can offer, any help you can give.

According to 1 Peter 3:7, your prayers can be hindered by lacking understanding toward your wife or by not honoring her. That's a powerful testimony to the emphasis God places on your role as a husband. Don't ignore the importance God places on your honoring and being understanding toward her.

God Desires Relationship

Sometimes the only thing hindering our prayers is our failure to pray, and this, too, reveals God. The essence and source of love, God wants to bless us. Yet, James writes, "you do not have, because you do not ask" (James 4:2). Omniscient, God knows what we need and desires to give it to us. Yet He waits. The fact that He waits for us to ask surely points to His longing to be in relationship with us.

Jesus says that if we've seen Him we've seen the Father (see John 14:9). And in His earthly ministry, Jesus revealed this divine trait, a desire for relationship, every day of His life. He touched people, literally and deeply emotionally. If you type *Jesus* and *touched* into a Bible search bar, you'll get lots of hits: people who were blind, lame, and even covered in oozing sores of leprosy. He touched them. That they were healed is usually our focus, but let's not lose sight of where Jesus focused—the interaction. Even when He was touched by a woman trying not to be seen, He insisted on interacting.

In Luke 8:43 we find a woman who has had a discharge of blood for twelve years that cannot be healed by any person or amount of money. But she believes she can be healed by simply touching Jesus' garment. And she is right! Communicating isn't necessary. He heals her. No interaction required.

However, Jesus insists on an interaction: "Jesus said, 'Who was it that touched me?'" (Luke 8:45). Now, He could have simply moved on, but no. Jesus waited for her to come to Him, to voluntarily interact.

She finally did. "When the woman saw that she was not hidden, she came trembling, and falling down before him declared in the presence of all the people why she had touched him, and how she had been immediately healed. And he said to her, 'Daughter, your faith has made you well; go in peace'" (Luke 8:47-48).

God knows what you need. He doesn't need you to pray. But relationship requires interaction—so He waits for you to pray.

Jesus knew who had touched Him and why. Don't gloss over this powerful truth. An interaction wasn't necessary for Him to know her needs or even to heal her. *But relationship does require interaction.*

Our faith is not about religion. It's not about answered prayer. Prayer is not about getting what we want or what we need. Our faith and our prayers are about relationship with God.

Make prayer a daily discipline and your knee-jerk reaction. Pray over concerns as they arise. Pray before big discussions—together. Pray when you're feeling irritable with each other. Pray together when you can't find the keys, don't feel great, or just aren't clicking.

More Prayer Together

About three years after our health scare with Patrick, we found out we were having a second child at the same time we learned that Mike's mother's cancer had returned. Once again we turned to prayer, prayers of praise for our second child and prayers of thanksgiving for Oneida's prior victory over cancer and supplication for her healing. However, her cancer metastasized to her liver, bones, and lungs. Just over three months later, she gained the greater victory. It wasn't the answer we wanted.

Three weeks after Oneida's funeral, my younger brother, Karl, just finishing a long day of work, headed to my mom's to pick up his daughters. As he drove over the railroad tracks at a rural, unmarked crossing, the train he must have never seen coming exploded through the driver's side of his vehicle. He died instantly.

After Karl's death and then his daughters' move far away from us, we all grieved. Only prayer could and did carry Mike and me through that time when we experienced that much pain and watched those we love deeply experience some of the most devastating consequences I've ever seen one death cause.

We prayed for my parents, whose youngest son had just been killed on the birth date of their oldest son, who had died as an infant. We prayed for my nieces who, at only five and seven, had just lost their father and then had to move more than eighteen hundred miles away from their schools, their friends, and our family.

The grief and loss weighed heavily on me. I was tormented by not being able to connect with those precious girls. I worried about the impact on our unborn child. We prayed for the well-being of all three.

In February, I delivered a healthy, happy baby boy, Colten. As for my nieces, seven years passed with little change. But finally, we clearly saw God answer our prayers by letting them come stay with us. They were able to reconnect with their family and old friends and make new friends. They came to know Jesus as Lord. We're still connected. I love them as much as I can imagine loving daughters.

Don't Stop

We have never prayed without God hearing us. We've never prayed without Him answering us one way or another. We've seen prayers answered powerfully. We've searched for answers to prayer without being able to see them. We've received answers of yes and answers of no. We've endured years of waiting and grieving. Someday, God will reveal how all His answers worked out for our good and His glory. Until then, we'll pray and build relationship with Him and know the peace that He alone gives.

Paul writes, "Do not be anxious about anything, but in everything by prayer and supplication with thanksgiving let your requests be made known to God" (Philippians 4:6). Be anxious about nothing. Be in prayer about everything. That's not hyperbole. That's a command. Don't wait for the moment that knocks you to your knees in fear. Don't let the times you can't see the answer to your prayers keep you from praying.

A Christian neglecting prayer is like a soldier ignoring his communication equipment on the battlefield and trying to fight an army on his own rather than signaling for help. Prayer reaches the ears of God, your defense and safety, your air support against the enemy. Prayer is the communication channel that reaches our Warrior-Father. Prayer is the place where we find peace even when the storm rages.

"This is the confidence that we have toward [God], that if we ask anything according to his will he hears us" (1 John 5:14).

God always hears. He always answers.

Countdown Journal

How will you make prayer an integral part of your life and marriage?

What are the specific times you will commit to praying together?

Anniversary Reflection

How has God shown Himself to you through your prayers, individually and as a couple, over the last year?

How can you deepen your time in prayer?

DAY 15

Submit One to the Other

A recurrent, long-standing battle between Mike and me revolved around leaving Crossett, Arkansas. I couldn't wait to leave. At first, I wanted to go back to Texas—only Texas would do. I had good reason. Crossett was tiny. We had to drive an hour to go to the ob-gyn or the pediatrician. All the things we both enjoyed—good restaurants, the movies, shopping—were at least an hour away. Employment opportunities were dying as the main employer closed down parts of their mill. The town was shrinking as people quickly moved away.

While Mike had no siblings, no nieces or nephews, my large family in Texas continued to grow. Now a widower, Mike's dad focused even more on his garden, his dog, and some new friendships. Many of Mike's hometown friends had gotten married, and their wives had become my friends. I worked hard to build strong relationships with them and with other teachers, but even they were beginning to move away. Those who still lived in Crossett were staying primarily because they had extended family who also lived there. As the members of our friend group had more and more children, their local extended families (understandably) became their primary focus, especially during holidays, leaving me feeling isolated in Crossett.

Mike loved to hunt—ducks and deer and squirrels and doves. When it wasn't hunting season, he liked to play tennis with his buddies. Those activities left me home alone with two children or found me traveling to Texas whenever school was on a break.

The disagreements brewed into resentment; arguments became increasingly insulting. Mike's seeming lack of concern for my loneliness hurt me deeply. He grew frustrated with my discontent. Anger bubbled up.

Learning to Submit

Every action you take that honors your wife honors Jesus. Every day that you live out your marriage as Christ intends, your marriage will reflect the redemption story of Christ and the church, of His pursuit and nurturing, of His passion and compassion, of His forgiving and restoring. You and your wife are both called to respond and act toward each other based on your relationship with Jesus. Colossians 3:18-19 calls for husbands to love and wives to submit.

Neither role, to love or to submit, is a one-sided command. In Ephesians, Paul writes of "submitting to one another out of reverence for Christ" (Ephesians 5:21). Husbands and wives, all Christians, are to submit one to another.

The command to love is certainly not one-sided either. Many verses command us to love one another, but Paul specifically instructs husbands how to love their wives: "Husbands, love your wives, as Christ loved the church and gave himself up for her, that he might sanctify her, having cleansed her by the washing of water with the word, so that he might present the church to himself in splendor, without spot or wrinkle or any such thing, that she might be holy and without blemish" (Ephesians 5:25-27).

As the husband, you're to love your bride as Jesus loves His bride; your wife is called to love you as she loves Jesus. A small syntactic difference but a significant difference in meaning exists in God's very clear instructions regarding how we're supposed to love each other. I don't claim to understand why the difference exists, and we may even struggle to explain the difference, but deep inside, on a spiritual level, we get it. It makes sense that men need to be told to love women as Jesus loves His bride, the church, and that women need to be told to love their husbands as they're to love the Lord.

Perhaps it's because the Holy Spirit knew that the enemy was building a cultural bias that would make loving husbands and respectful wives the butt of almost every joke and would attack those roles as being demeaning. The Holy Spirit also knew that men might think it easier to die for their wives than to give themselves up for them, to work to sanctify them, to focus on their spiritual growth.

Maybe the passage was written this way because many men need encouragement to lead and love. Even though probably every bridegroom has said—and believed—that he would give his life to protect his wife, those same men have had a hard time giving up a few moments to carry their dirty clothes to the hamper. The man who believes he would sacrifice his body to protect his wife will often spend hours in the gym building that body while his wife feels neglected at home. The husband who promises to protect his wife may refuse to stand up to his children when they smart off to her. The man willing to suffer a beating for her explodes with anger when she asks him to do something that disrupts his downtime.

Scripture is clear that marriage is a place of mutual submission and love.

A Word About Abuse

Let's be clear. Wives don't have to stand for and passively accept abuse. Love doesn't overlook or ignore sin. Submission does not mean glossing over sin, let alone giving way to it. The commands for respect, submission, and self-sacrifice in no way condone violence or abuse of any kind.

No one should suffer abuse, especially in the home. Domestic violence is a dangerous, devastating, and destructive sin. The first step in the face of domestic abuse is to protect those at risk of harm. We must take a stand for those being hurt. It's a sad truth that some marriages can be places of abuse. *God forbid it ever come at your hand.*

For most of us, the struggle is much more insidious. We need to be reminded that we're breaking the covenant when we refuse to meet each other's needs, even if the needs of the other person are needs we don't have, don't understand, or are hard for us to satisfy. We're breaking the covenant if we avoid the conversation when the other person needs it, even if it may develop into an argument. We're breaking the covenant if we force the conversation at a time when the other person doesn't want to have it.

If she wants to have a talk and you're living out the covenant, you'll give up your right *not* to talk. If she doesn't want to talk right then and you can delay the conversation, you're not living the covenant if you force the conversation. If it matters to her and it can honor God, you'll make a sacrifice to make it happen. If you're at odds with her, you'll seek reconciliation by sacrificing yourself. Yes, she's called to live up to her end of the covenant, but that's God's calling to her—never your justification for shirking your calling to love your wife as Christ loves the church.

Honoring Our Commitment

When we both honor our commitment, life gets better. Tough times are bearable; good times are fantastic. When one of us doesn't honor our commitment and the other does, we can survive and trust the Lord to sustain us. The burden is on the Lord to soften the heart; the job of breaking down walls belongs to the Holy Spirit.

When we're failing our covenant or justifying our actions by the other's misbehavior, Satan takes a stronghold. Needs go unmet. Children lose security. The marriage takes a beating. The Lord is not honored.

We've been there. At times, each of us has failed the relationship, failed God, faulted the other, and wounded our loved ones. We've refused to sacrifice. We've kept a false score. We also have, more rarely, found ourselves on the other end of the spectrum—doing more, working harder, feeling less guilty.

Mike and I used to not fight well. Mike hated (and still hates) conflict and prefers to avoid it—at almost any cost. I'm direct. I tend to think that logic will prevail. However, it became clear early on that if Mike wanted or didn't want to do something, my expressed opinion didn't carry a lot of weight. He would listen to me talk and seem to really take in what I was saying. He would hear me complain and often placate me by agreeing with my view. But the situation would go unchanged.

I truly believed that if he really understood my side, the situation would change, so I would go at it again in a new way, with a new analogy or better example. He would listen and often agree to do something different. And time would pass. Then I'd get hurt, frustrated, and finally angry.

We've tried our hardest, and then we've quit—sometimes within the same hour. I've said I will never leave and then turned around and packed my stuff—in the same night. We've been in that negative cycle and stayed there far too long at times.

You may find yourself feeling similar negative emotions. Our hope is that the lessons we've learned over thirty years can help you avoid some of the pitfalls, or at least get out of them faster.

When you feel you've forgiven more than is reasonable and done more than your share, remind yourself that Jesus left His throne, humbled Himself by coming to humanity as a baby, lived a blameless life, and then bore your sins at Calvary. We rise or fall before Him alone.

Our Father truly does make "all things work together for good, for those who are called according to his purpose" (Romans 8:28). "All things" means all things, including our fights and arguments and even our sins.

The good news is that God has a good plan. On this side of the fighting, Mike and I love each other more truly and deeply than ever. We still mess up; the consequences still hurt us; but God faithfully defeats Satan daily. He continues to make "all things work together for good." He will work all things together for your good, too, because you also love Him and are called according to His purpose.

Jesus was not only willing to die for us but also to live for us. Leaving behind heaven and glory and the Father, He lived a human life for us. He gave up heaven and all its joys for us. He labored as a carpenter so that He could better understand us. He suffered spite and betrayal for us even though He was perfectly blameless. The disrespect and hurtful actions He suffered were not in response to some pain or sin He committed. The consequences He faced were not due to His mistakes or behavior. None of His actions were flawed or sinful. Although He was and always is perfect, His best friends, His bride (the church), you, and I disrespect, neglect, and betray Him. He knew we would. He knows we will. Yet He gave up everything and faced total public humiliation for us.

God works all things together for good—even our mistakes. God heals, restores, and redeems.

Jesus' very best friends and worst enemies both treated Him horribly, yet He continued up to Golgotha. Peter cursed Him and denied even knowing Him in the courtyard in the presence of many people. How did Jesus respond? He simply looked at Peter. Then He died for Peter.

Then—and this is truly one of the most poignant events in the Gospels, epitomizing the potency of grace and mercy—Jesus sought Peter on the seashore, where He, the One who had been wronged, initiated reconciliation.

Jesus, risen from the dead, fixed breakfast for Peter and several others. Then He initiated reconciliation with Peter, the one who had denied Him three times. He didn't wait for Peter to apologize.

He didn't ask for an apology. He asked Peter to affirm his love for Him—three times. And each time, He gave Peter encouragement to put his love into action. In the very next moments, after having just experienced the restorative grace of Jesus, Peter turned his focus to someone else:

> Peter turned and saw the disciple whom Jesus loved following them, the one who also had leaned back against him during the supper and had said, "Lord, who is it that is going to betray you?" When Peter saw him, he said to Jesus, "Lord, what about this man?" Jesus said to him, "If it is my will that he remain until I come, what is that to you? You follow me!"
>
> JOHN 21:20-22

We do the same thing, don't we? The Word tells us how to express our love for God, how to put that love into action. The Word instructs, "Love your wives, as Christ loved the church" (Ephesians 5:25). Before we even face the first challenge to that effort, almost before we hear the end of the Lord's exhortation, we say, *Lord, what about her? What should she be doing?*

Jesus spoke to Peter, and His words speak to us: *What is that to you? You follow Me!*

Don't get distracted by what your wife should and shouldn't do. Her actions neither dictate nor justify yours. Jesus reminded Peter right there on the seashore not to focus on what another person should do or not do.

As a husband, you're making a covenant with God to love your wife as Christ loves the church. You're entering into an agreement that you'll do good regardless of what happens, even when things are bad. No matter what your wife does or is called to do, Jesus says, *What is that to you? You follow Me!*

Countdown Journal

How will you feed, protect, and nurture your future wife as yourself?

What will you be willing to do for her—literally and daily?

Anniversary Reflection

What scores have been kept that need to be erased? What forgiveness needs to be extended?

DAY 14

Forsake All Others

On a Wednesday night, I found my marriage dying in our bathroom. As the kids and I walked in from Bible class, I called Mike's name but heard no answer. The kids had been laughing and teasing one another on the way home and continued their loud banter. "Settle down and take your baths," I called.

I hurried through the bedroom toward the bathroom. Mike was standing in the bathroom, still dressed for work, just closing the linen cabinet door. "Hey, there you are," I said. "Did you just get home? What a day!"

"Just a few minutes ago," he said, stepping out of my way. "How was Bible class? Are the kids excited about tomorrow?"

"They couldn't be any more excited. We may never get them to bed." I watched him loosen his tie and hang it in his closet. He looked tired.

"I'll go check on them and see if I can get them headed that way," he said as he moved out of the bathroom. "Want to watch television with me while you work?"

"Sure," I murmured as he walked out.

I couldn't put my finger on it, but something was wrong. The conversation echoed the ones we had almost every night. It had been a hard year though; our lives had changed in ways we had never expected. We had a new house, I had a new job, and he had a more demanding position at work. I had worked hard to give him the downtime he needed in the evenings and on the weekends by taking the kids with me to grocery shop or run errands. I planned all-day playdates on Saturdays while he worked in the yard so he could enjoy his time with his John Deere. Despite my efforts, he seemed ever more tired, burdened, and irritable.

With no real reason or forethought, I opened the door to the linen cabinet he had just closed. His small, blue cell phone lay just inside the door, almost completely tucked behind the stack of bath towels. My heart sank, and the weight of it in the pit of my stomach caused a wave of nausea.

I remember wondering at the sudden feeling of panic. Why had just the sight of a cell phone, oddly out of its normal place, made my world tremble? For some inexplicable reason, I picked up the phone and scrolled through the list of numbers dialed. Only four appeared, and it at once struck me that there should have been a list of the last ten numbers. He had deleted six of them. Alarm bells went off in my mind even as I wondered at my own reaction. I sat down on the toilet seat and laid the phone in my lap.

The heartbeat of our marriage seemed to be ebbing away as an indiscernible enemy tightened his grip around the throat of our one flesh.

As I walked through the hall, passed the kitchen, and entered the living room, the silence that had engulfed me in the bathroom faded beneath the din of television noise, boys' laughter, and the *Roaring Lambs* CD playing upstairs. As I sat beside him, he raised his arm to the back of the couch so I could snuggle in beside him. The action almost knocked the breath out of me.

"Who were you talking to on the phone?" I asked.

"When?"

"Don't do that," I said quietly. "I *know* you were talking to someone and don't want me to know who it was. You've deleted the last numbers called." I could barely hear my voice over my own thoughts, which were confused: *Know? What do I know? I don't know anything.*

"What are you talking about?" His question echoed my own thoughts, but beneath his words lay a mixture of anger, surprise, and something almost like smugness. If I had felt confused by my own reaction, his response convinced me that I had stumbled onto some horrible truth.

"Who was on the phone?"

"I had called you to see if you were close to home," he said, "but I hung up when I heard the garage door open. What's your problem?"

He continued watching television, deliberately avoiding my eyes. I went back to the bathroom and the phone. My cell phone number was the last showing on the short list. Maybe I was overreacting. *Of course I am*, I told myself.

As the struggle in my heart continued, I mindlessly scrolled through the menu. The word *Messages* appeared. I had never paid much attention to that option. We had never added text messaging to our phones.

I selected the prompt anyway and then chose Inbox; it was empty. I began to relax and feel a little foolish. Then I selected Outbox. I frowned at my own doubts and the corresponding compulsion to be sure there was nothing behind my fears.

One message appeared: "I long for you." The message waited to be sent to scorpiogirl. I am not scorpiogirl. I read it again and searched for a way to discover the identity of scorpiogirl. My mind reeled with panic. *What does this mean? Is this some kind of horoscope thing? What is a scorpiogirl? Who calls herself something like that?*

My world had turned upside down in just minutes. I struggled to think clearly. Part of me wanted to toss the phone back where I found it, pretending I had never opened the text message he had been writing. My eyes burned; I gagged on bile churning in my throat.

I returned to the couch and handed him his phone with the text message still displayed.

"Who is it?" I asked as the turmoil inside me roiled. I couldn't believe we were having this conversation. How was this our life? Could this man, one of the most loyal friends I've known, be involved with someone else at any level?

"What does it matter?" he countered. "Don't do this in here. The kids will hear you."

"Why are you worrying about the kids now? They'll have to know soon enough."

He rose and walked toward our room. He turned back toward me as he beckoned me to join him. "Come in here at least."

I followed him through the bedroom and into our bathroom. His face showed almost no emotion, perhaps a hint of annoyance or anger. Sitting on the edge of our bathtub, I felt a strong urge to lay my face against the hard, cold surface. I felt sick.

As I sat on the edge of the tub, my head in my hands, I felt the lifeblood of our marriage draining onto the bathroom floor. He leaned against the wall and said in a monotone, "What do you want me to say? I'm sorry?" He paused long enough that I wondered if he really expected an answer. "I am sorry," he finally continued. "I didn't mean for this to happen."

Setting Boundaries

I'll tell more of that story later. But it highlights the fact that one of the most important disciplines you and your fiancée need to learn as you enter marriage is how to establish healthy boundaries with members of the opposite sex—in your case, with women other than your wife. While you'll continue to have friends and colleagues who are women, as a man who respects his role as a husband and wants to honor and protect his wife, you must set clear boundaries for those interactions and diligently adhere to them. Please know that this chapter is included out of love and because of my personal, painful experience, not because of doubt about your commitment or love for each other.

I can't imagine being described by God for all history as a person after God's own heart. Can you imagine having such a heart that God would memorialize you in Scripture that way? That's exactly how God's Word describes King David, yet he committed adultery that led to murder. The truth is that every person, no matter how strong his or her convictions about monogamy, is in danger of becoming emotionally or physically intimate with another person unless strong boundaries are set and enforced on one's thoughts and actions.

Dedicated Christians can, and have, let actions that could be argued to be completely innocent start them down a slippery slope that has led to sexual sin. Most of us have not had anyone teach us to draw boundaries to protect ourselves and our marriages from infidelity or how much damage not having proper boundaries can cause. In fact, the world around us ridicules almost every hint of propriety and sexualizes every aspect of life. Lack of guidance, immaturity, easy access (almost *unavoidable* access) to porn, naïveté about relationships, and arrogance about our own ability to resist temptation all place us at great risk of cheating and destroying our marriages.

Our culture glamorizes sex outside marriage, opposes limitations of any kind, and ridicules the concepts of purity and monogamy. Paul makes it clear that this is not God's perspective. In Ephesians 5, he writes that "sexual immorality and all impurity or covetousness must not even be named among you." He adds that neither "filthiness nor foolish talk nor crude joking" should be tolerated (Ephesians 5:3-4).

We live in a culture that idolizes sex, views purity as impossible, and ridicules anyone who disagrees.

From God's opening statement in Genesis that a man and woman should forsake all others to Jesus' reteaching God's plan for marriage in Matthew, Scripture makes it clear that marriage is a holy union between one man and one woman for life.

How is it, then, that nearly 10 percent of people in a recent study of Americans believed that adultery is acceptable?[1]

Focus on the Family notes that most polls report that more than one-third of men and one-quarter of women admit to having committed adultery at least once.[2]

Research by Barna reveals that more than half of practicing Christians view pornography "with some level of frequency."[3]

Don't be deceived. Jesus condemns it all as adultery: "I say to you that everyone who looks at a woman with lustful intent has already committed adultery with her in his heart" (Matthew 5:28). He doesn't mince words. He makes it clear that we're to create powerful boundaries.

Nor does He hesitate to indicate how seriously we should take the prevention of this sin:

> "If your right eye causes you to sin, tear it out and throw it away. For it is better that you lose one of your members than that your whole body be thrown into hell. And if your right hand causes you to sin, cut it off and throw it away. For it is better that you lose one of your members than that your whole body go into hell."
>
> MATTHEW 5:29-30

Yet not only are those same one in three men and one in four women walking around with both eyes functioning and both hands fully intact, but they're also logged on practically all day and most of the night without any internet filters on their phones, their home computers, or their work computers.

Jesus commands us to cut off and throw away anything that causes us to sin. If our electronics aren't smoldering in an ash heap, at the very least they should have filters installed that prevent access to questionable sites and send a history of everything we view to an accountability partner—a filter that won't allow us to bypass it. Despite what most of the world will tell you about your right to privacy, Mike and I believe strongly that wives should have free access to their husbands' electronics, social media, and email accounts, and husbands should have free access to all the same technology belonging to their wives.

God's call to holiness and honor takes the standard to a different level—a level that requires strong boundaries; boundaries to help you control your own body in holiness; boundaries that honor God; boundaries that honor your wife.

You and your fiancée need to set such boundaries in place. How do you want her to protect herself from the risk of inappropriate advances by men, from the lure of porn? What boundaries will honor you and protect her? Those boundaries are, at the minimum, the same ones you should set. (For more on setting these kinds of healthy boundaries, see the book *Hedges*, written by Jerry B. Jenkins and published by Focus on the Family.)

The first sin began with "a casual conversation" filled with lies challenging the first boundary set by God. The same step leads to broken marriage vows.

Mike and I don't take this stand from a moral high ground. We take this stand from our redeemed status, hoping to keep you from the devastation of adultery. Believe me when I say this: No matter how loyal you are, no matter how loyal she is—adultery can happen in your marriage if you don't draw clear and powerful boundaries. It happens in millions of marriages—even in Christian homes. It happened in ours.

The Early Part of Our Story

Mike and I had finally reached a compromise on the issue that had festered in our marriage for more than a decade. We had found a beautiful lot on a bayou forty-five minutes south of Crossett and only ten minutes away from an amazing Christian school our kids loved—and twenty minutes from a theater, shopping, and a whole new slate of restaurants. The move put us only thirty minutes from White's Ferry Road Church of Christ (WFR), a congregation of believers we had quickly grown to love that was led by a godly group of elders. WFR had a strong youth group and children's

Bible-class program. The ministers taught Scripture and focused on the gospel.

Excited about all the opportunities, especially the school and the church, we built the house of our dreams on the outskirts of Monroe, Louisiana.

Actively involved in a church we loved, living in a place we had chosen together, deeply grateful for the family God had given us, *our marriage crumbled.* There was no blowup, no big crisis, no defining moment that caused the collapse. Instead, our marriage's foundation—weak due to years of poor boundaries and disagreements swept under the rug in the name of keeping the peace—quietly cracked under the weight of too many distractions.

The slippery slope to infidelity almost always begins with friendship—just conversation. For that reason, every conversation with a woman other than a close relative needs to be scrutinized. Creating a strong boundary between you and a person of the opposite sex means drawing a line so that flirtatious comments or jokes, let alone anything more intimate, are virtually impossible.

Those boundaries should address how you'll avoid spending time alone with another woman. How will you handle dinners, lunches, car rides, business trips, and work meetings? How do you want your wife to handle interactions with other men?

> **God's will is not just for you to avoid adultery; His will is for your marriage to exemplify holiness.**

Would it hurt you if you found she was hanging around the coffee counter at work regularly just to talk with a particular male coworker? Would it bother you if she were regularly messaging an old boyfriend just to see what he was up to now? Would you be worried if she were talking to another man about struggles with you? If you answered no to any of these, *you need to ask why you aren't being honest with yourself.* And if you would be bothered if your wife did any of these things, you should never allow yourself to do them either.

First Thessalonians 4:3-5 says, "This is the will of God, your sanctification: that you abstain from sexual immorality; that each one of you know how to control his own body in holiness and honor, not in the passion of lust like the Gentiles who do not know God."

Any friendship with another woman should include and honor your wife. To many people, especially in our culture, these boundaries seem extreme, but protecting the marriage covenant requires extreme diligence. This stance often stirs up defensiveness, derision, and even charges of sexism. Indeed, any kind of boundary or self-denial creates a backlash in a world bent on self-expression and indulgence.

But don't let the world skew your compass. Focus on Scripture and surround yourself with godly people who will challenge you to pursue holiness, who have found freedom in Jesus and are living in the power of the Holy Spirit. Seek out men who aren't afraid of friction, men willing to stand strong for and with you—even if that means standing against you. "Iron sharpens iron, and one man sharpens another" (Proverbs 27:17).

Ponder the paths you will and won't walk, the boundaries you won't cross. Keep your heart focused on Jesus as your first love and your wife as your life partner. Don't compare your wife with other women, even fictional ones! Covetousness begins with comparison. Bitterness begins with a negative thought. Fight the world's urging to critique and find fault with your wife.

> Let all bitterness and wrath and anger and clamor and slander be put away from you, along with all malice. Be kind to one another, tenderhearted, forgiving one another, as God in Christ forgave you.
>
> EPHESIANS 4:31-32

Countdown Journal

What boundaries will you build together to honor each other and prevent even a hint of sexual immorality?

What measures will you take to protect yourself and your wife online, on your phones, and at work?

Anniversary Reflection

What men in your life have proved to be trustworthy accountability partners?

What boundaries in your life are helping your marriage exemplify holiness? What boundaries need to change?

DAY 13

Find Your Worth in God

After Adam and Eve sinned, God told Adam, "Because you have listened to the voice of your wife and have eaten of the tree of which I commanded you, 'You shall not eat of it,' cursed is the ground because of you; in pain you shall eat of it all the days of your life; thorns and thistles it shall bring forth for you; and you shall eat the plants of the field. By the sweat of your face you shall eat bread" (Genesis 3:17-19). I've seen this curse borne out in my husband's life. It has empowered a damaging, repetitive battle in our marriage.

From the time we married, I had desperately wanted to leave Crossett. Mike knew it. I believed that if I really mattered to him, he would move. He, on the other hand, saw expanding authority, a better position, and a growing salary at the bank in Crossett as the way to provide for our family. He had worked hard to succeed, and the idea of changing jobs seemed like an unnecessary risk. Meanwhile, my insistence on moving had planted a seed in his mind that he was failing at making me happy.

The more I doubted Mike's love for me and my worth to him, the harder I worked to make it (and me) matter to him. The more I hurt, the more I tried to make him understand. The more we argued, the more he doubted his ability to make me happy. Over time, he turned his focus more to the people and place that made him feel successful. The enemy's temptation gained a foothold as we both looked for our worth in the wrong places: me looking for it in Mike; Mike looking for it in coworkers and work.

On a deeper and even more subconscious level, Mike, like many men, struggles with laying down his life as Christ lay down His life for His bride. Mike had been raised in Crossett; had grown up with the friends, teammates, hunting buddies, and former girlfriends who still lived there; lived close to his parents; had found success at the bank; and still enjoyed the remnants of high school glory days. He had never really considered that staying in that place, tied to all those liaisons and working at the bank where he felt secure and admired, might not be God's plan.

The Meaning of the Curse

Don't minimize the first part of what God said to Adam: "Because you have listened to the voice of your wife" (Genesis 3:17). Adam wasn't deceived; he was influenced by his wife to do what he knew was wrong (see 1 Timothy 2:14). Letting his desire to make his wife happy take precedence over God's clear instructions led to the sin that brought a curse on his calling to work.

> You need the Holy Spirit to help you resist finding your value in work or play or in pleasing your wife rather than in God alone.

Not only does God know what's good for us and give us every good thing, but God also knows how sin changes us, how it twists and damages our lives, how it turns our hearts away from Him. When Adam and Eve sinned, the curse of sin warped the state of the world, altering what God had intended for us.

For men, sin brought grief into work, opposition between toil and progress, the soil and growth. What was good became difficult. What had been pleasurable and easy was now made to be burdensome and hard.

Even worse, since the fall, what God intends to be holy and uplifting has had opportunity to become the idol we turn to for our self worth, an idol that distorts the truth and takes control of our lives. Women tend to look to husbands (or boyfriends) to find self-worth, and they also tend to make their children the center of their lives. Husbands look to success at work and play, the paycheck or the scoreboard, to find self-worth, and they also tend to justify the right- or wrongness of their actions by the happiness or unhappiness of their wife or girlfriend.

You're called to love your wife as Christ loves the church, to love her as your own body. Remember that when the enemy attacks he tries to twist the truth. He'll tempt you to love your wife more than Jesus. He'll tempt you to use her to love yourself. He'll urge you to keep her happy even if it dishonors God. He'll convince you that avoiding a fight is more important than resolving an issue. The enemy wants you to fight with her but not for her, to find your self-worth in her mood rather than in God's calling.

The enemy tries to distort our view of work, too. We're called to work; work is honorable and honors God. But when the lies of the enemy attack our hearts, work becomes the god we honor and serve. Instead of finding our self-worth in Jesus and doing whatever we can to reflect His image to others, we find our self-worth in what we can do and base our self-image on how others see us. Keeping your self-worth rooted in God's image requires time in the Word, prayers for wisdom, and being accountable to mature, godly people.

Your True Source of Worth

Just as he has done from the beginning, the enemy will twist the truth to lure people—including you and your wife—away from the will of God. Only He belongs at the center of our lives. Only He should be loved with all our hearts, souls, minds, and strength.

You're called to cleave to your wife, to lay your life down for her, to submit your own desires to hers so long as it honors God. But the enemy will tempt you to love your wife *more* than Christ. He'll urge you to keep your wife happy even if it dishonors God.

If creating an idol of your wife doesn't work, the enemy will tempt you to be disrespectful to her because she isn't living up to your idol standards. The enemy would love to see you become bitter toward your wife, to feel contempt for her. The enemy will work hard to convince you that being right is more important than resolving an issue. He wants you to fight with, not for, your wife.

This is where Mike and I landed. We were fighting each other over where we would live. We were fighting because we were seeking our worth outside our relationships with God. We were fighting against each other because we were believing the lies of the enemy.

We eventually moved to that beautiful lot on a bayou with a big new house, a loving church family, and a strong school for our children. But even as everything we wanted for our family fell into place, our marriage was suffering. We loved God and believed in Jesus as Lord. But we had divided hearts. Rather than being one flesh with one God, we were still two people with our allegiances torn between God and an idol—each other. This resulted in a broken marriage bleeding out on the bathroom floor.

Many nights during that time when my marriage was dying, I couldn't sleep. I would wait until everyone else was asleep and then shut our bedroom door, go into our bathroom, and shut and lock that door behind me. Then I'd walk into my closet, closing that door behind me, and sit on the floor, burrowing behind the coats hanging on the back wall. There I could cry and pray without risking my children hearing me.

I felt like we had failed. Our marriage was collapsing, and we couldn't see any way forward. All Mike and I knew was that we didn't want our children to know the insecurity I had felt as a child when my parents had threatened over and over to separate. But we didn't know how we could stay married.

Mike and I both agreed to keep the crisis as private as possible to protect each other, to protect our children, and to give us time to decide what we could and should do. We both struggled with isolation, shame, and doubt and with wounds that made small slights feel like gut punches. Almost no one even knew what had happened let alone understood what we were enduring.

We agreed on very little during that time except that God alone really knew what had happened and that only He could get us through it. As we read in Psalms, "in [His] book were written, every one of them, the days that were formed for me, when as yet there was none of them" (Psalm 139:16). He alone knew then and knows now the plans He has for me, for Mike, for our family.

We didn't know how we could stay married or whether we would, but we did know that our Father had a plan to prosper and not harm us (see Jeremiah 29:11). We could trust that. I did know, even there in that closet, that God saw me. I knew His will was for my marriage to be permanent, but I also knew that people have free will and sin lies at the door.

One night as I cried in the closet, God revealed that He saw me for exactly who I was, where I was. He reminded me that I'm His child. He loves me not because of who I am but because I'm His. In that moment of feeling fully seen by Him, I became completely aware that I was fully loved by Him. And because He loved me, I couldn't stay where I was but was compelled to draw closer and closer to Him, to become more and more like Him.

> **Regardless of anyone's feelings—your own or others'—your worth has been solidly established and will never change: You are a son of the most high God.**

Align your beliefs about being a husband with God's truth. You were created for the good works God prepared for you before you existed (see Ephesians 2:8-10). You're doing those good works when you love your wife well. However, your worth is immeasurably greater than your role as a husband or worker can ever create. You're worth the death of Jesus Christ because God chose you. You've put on Christ; His image is imprinted on you. Your worth is found in the price God paid for you.

Your self-image is rooted in the image of Christ, that which reflects the Father, and in God's love and the blood of Christ. Your worth is the worth of a son of God, both the Son who died for you and the son He made you.

Countdown Journal

What tempts you to find your self-worth outside God?

How will you battle the tendency to find your worth through the work of your hands?

How will you battle the tendency to try to please your wife more than God?

Anniversary Reflection

How have you dealt with your desire to prove your worth through work (or play)?

How have you managed your tendency to try to keep your wife happy at the expense of your calling as a son of God?

How can you best honor God in your marriage?

DAY 12

Help Her Find Her Worth in God

Like most dating and engaged couples, Mike and I found that romance and affection bubbled up naturally. Mike believed these things shouldn't take extra effort. As time passed and we settled into the routine of marriage, however, he began to have less energy for them. Work demands and parenting took more space and effort, and he maintained his focus on hunting and tennis with his buddies, but our relationship lost ground.

As Mike's attention waned, my focus shifted to that void. When I expressed my hurt and disappointment, he became defensive. His behavior continued with him blissfully and, in his own estimation now looking back, selfishly unaware of the impact on me. A common cycle that strikes many marriages began and soon became entrenched in ours:

- He would do or say something hurtful to me, maybe naïvely or ignorantly or even selfishly.
- I would hide the hurt in an attempt to not nag.
- If he was even aware of any possible concern, he would take my lack of complaint as confirmation that his choice was just fine.

- He would do or say a similar thing again and sometimes take a bit more license.
- I would try not to get into a fight with him but feel more hurt and angry.
- Then the pattern would repeat, digging the rut deeper.
- My hurt (expressed in more and more anger) would break through any concern about not nagging.
- I had plenty of so-called proof of his neglect and insults.
- He had plenty of proof that I had an anger problem.

Finding Her Worth

Your wife, like you, needs to find her worth in bearing the image of God. And like you, she can easily be tripped up by the lies of the enemy. Since Eve fell into sin, women have tended to find their worth in the reflection of themselves in their husbands and in their success as mothers.

Jesus calls the enemy of our souls "the father of lies" (John 8:44). He lies about God. He lies about the consequences of sin. He lies about God's calling for wives and mothers.

These lies are an unholy strategy he uses successfully with many women. God created marriage and motherhood to be both a calling and a blessing. In both roles, women honor God and His design. However, when the lies of the enemy attack our hearts, we lose perspective, trading truth for falsehood.

The curses are not God's pronouncement on the world; they are the consequences of sin.

Instead of marriage and motherhood being the way women serve and honor God, if they listen to the liar, one or both of these things will become the god they honor and serve. You'll need the Holy Spirit to empower you to honor God in your work and influence without seeking your self-worth there. Your wife will need the Holy Spirit to help her resist looking for her self-worth in you or your children.

Our Story Continued

So how have Mike and I tackled these lies? We've gone to counseling, prayed separately and together, and spent hours and hours reframing our thoughts. Now we can see those times described at the start of this chapter as times we did not fight well. We can see in them choices we made that violated our commitment to God, rather than simply being personal attacks. While we don't minimize in any way the sinful choices we made that had devastating consequences, we do see how much we were both deceived.

Only by looking intently into the Word as the mirror for our souls can we keep our perspective in accord with Jesus' will for our lives. Your wife will spend the majority of her life working to provide care for you and your children, working to help others, working to stay healthy, and even, I hope, working in ministry. She will be tempted, over and over, to base her self-worth on how well she does those things. Pray for her, and help her fight the lies the enemy plants about her role as wife and mother. Be careful not to contribute to the lies.

> Satan works hard to turn the blessings of God into idols that come between us and Him.

The first step in helping her find her worth in God is to be sure *you* find *yours* in God. If you allow her happiness to become more important to you than God in any way, you'll be feeding the curse that pulls at her—a desire for undue influence over you. Keeping God first means refusing anything, even your wife if she seeks to take God's place in your life, if it would draw you away from Him or rival His place in your heart. Ideally you and your wife will encourage each other to find your self-esteem in God and not to believe that your worth is found anywhere else.

If you have children, you'll discover a love that can't be experienced any other way. They're a blessing from God. But just as the enemy does with everything, he'll try to use your children against you, to lure you away from God or to get you to betray your role as a husband. Don't give the enemy a foothold by allowing your life to be dictated by the tempers of toddlers or teens.

Beware Little Foxes

My marriage didn't collapse because of big issues. Neither of us went into it without genuine, deep commitment. Mike is honestly one of the most loyal, steadfast people I've ever known. We didn't have big warning signs or embrace sinful thoughts or actions. We spent a lot of time together, raised our children with shared values, attended church as a family, helped others, and loved God.

In Song of Solomon 2:15, the wise man Solomon warns about "little foxes that spoil the vineyards." And little foxes left uncaught eroded our relationship almost completely undetected. We didn't resolve issues.

Mike tends to avoid. I tend to be direct. He tended to do what made him comfortable regardless of what I said. I tended to do what I believed needed to be done even if he wouldn't. In most cases, I would just accept what he preferred, even if we both knew it wasn't what was best, as long as it didn't affect the kids—until my hurt turned to anger and the anger turned to resentment.

Those little foxes ate away at the roots of our marriage, actually hiding behind its good fruit. We spent a lot of time together, but we usually did what Mike enjoyed and spent time with his family. We raised our children with shared values, but I was quick to take the lead on discipline, and Mike found it easier to let me. We attended church as a family but didn't study or pray together as a couple privately. We helped others but usually separately because it was easier that way; we both had our own styles. We loved God but didn't apply His Word to our intimate relationship. We were image bearers of God but were looking for our worth in each other.

Over time, it became a pattern that caused me to stay busy and distracted and left him disconnected from our relationship and feeling more valued by his friends and coworkers. I began feeling unloved, and he began feeling disrespected.

Satan is a powerful deceiver, a threatening adversary, but you can resist him. When you resist him, God promises victory. Peter writes in 1 Peter 5:8-10:

> Be sober-minded; be watchful. Your adversary the devil prowls around like a roaring lion, seeking someone to devour. Resist him, firm in your faith, knowing that the same kinds of suffering are being experienced by your brotherhood throughout the world. And after you have suffered a little while, the God of all grace, who has called you to his eternal glory in Christ, will himself restore, confirm, strengthen, and establish you.

Be alert, watchful for signs that the enemy is gaining a foothold in your heart or in your wife's or creating disconnection in your marriage. Watch for signs that either of you is finding your self-worth anywhere but in God. Watch for little foxes that erode your relationship. Be willing to fight for each other. Stand firm in your faith and your calling in Christ.

God saved our marriage from a roaring lion. Mike had to turn his heart away from the lies of the enemy, and I had to turn my heart away from other lies of that same enemy. I wish I could say it was over as suddenly as it began. The infidelity was short-lived, but that brief, sinful involvement required an enormous and lengthy holy intervention. God worked on us individually, with us as a couple, and through others (like our counselors, Alan and Lisa Robertson). He kept working on us—to restore, confirm, strengthen, and establish us.

Never Forget

Never forget where your worth is properly found. It's found in bearing the image of God, in the relationship you have with the One who created you. Likewise, your wife's worth is not found in the role God has given her as a wife or mother or worker or friend. Her worth, too, is found in bearing God's image.

So be the husband your wife needs, the one who lays down his own will, his life, for her. And help her find her worth in God, in being God's workmanship created in Christ Jesus for the good works planned for her before either of you existed (see Ephesians 2:10).

Countdown Journal

What tempts your bride to find her worth outside God?

How will you help her battle those tendencies?

Anniversary Reflection

What idol has the enemy tempted you to build in your life over the past year?

How will you and your wife tear down idols and help each other love God with all your hearts, souls, minds, and strength?

DAY 11

Focus on Reconciliation

When Mike and I were at the lowest point in our marriage, I struggled with forgiveness. I wanted to assign blame. I felt angry, hurt, betrayed, confused, vengeful, and sad. Only when I turned my focus fully to my relationship with Jesus could I find peace.

One night as I cried and prayed, I recounted all the ways I had been wronged. I'm not clear in hindsight on all I listed, and I can promise you that knowing he had kissed the other woman wasn't the worst item, but I can still hear myself saying, *How could he do that? How could he betray me with a kiss?* And as clear now as it was then, I remember hearing a gruff, agonized voice say, "Judas, would you betray the Son of Man with a kiss?" (Luke 22:48).

Jesus knew exactly how I felt. He knew exactly what was going on in my life. He chose Judas knowing he would betray Him. He loved Judas knowing Judas would betray the Lord who loved him.

Jesus also knows how I've betrayed Him—how my sins nailed

Him to the cross, how my salvation required His pain, how my righteousness hinged on His dying in my place.

In that moment, with the words of Jesus ringing in my ears, I knew I would forgive Mike.

"Forgive us our sins, as we forgive those who sin against us" (Luke 11:4, NLT).

In that moment, I didn't know what would happen to our marriage. I would forgive Mike, but whether our marriage would be saved would be up to both of us.

Over a period of months, Mike and I were in counseling with a couple named Alan and Lisa Robertson. After that, we both were fully committed to restoring our marriage. Mike had ended all contact with the other woman. We also went to counseling with a licensed therapist for quite a while and have returned when needed.

Reconciliation in Marriage

Whenever you're challenged by your wife's behavior, you're called to react as you would to the Lord.

You'll blow it. I've certainly blown it. When you do, you're commanded to go and seek reconciliation with your wife. It's not optional. You were created to hold fast to her, to pursue her hard. Pursuing reconciliation with her is one of the ways you do that.

You need to have godly people around you who love you both enough (and whom you love enough) to help each of you when you can't work through a problem privately, just between the two of you. Seek out godly men to help you through the tough times, to encourage you as a man of God. As you grow in your marriage, intentionally build healthy relationships with other Jesus-following couples.

When an issue arises between you and your wife, whether you're hurt or she's hurt, you're called to model Christ. Here are a few

Scriptures especially poignant in teaching you what to do when your wife isn't doing what you think she should:

1. Pray without quarreling.
   - "I desire then that in every place the men should pray, lifting holy hands without anger or quarreling" (1 Timothy 2:8).
   - "Confess your sins to one another and pray for one another, that you may be healed. The prayer of a righteous person has great power as it is working" (James 5:16).
2. Act honorably.
   - "Repay no one evil for evil, but give thought to do what is honorable in the sight of all" (Romans 12:17).
3. Live peaceably.
   - "If possible, so far as it depends on you, live peaceably with all" (Romans 12:18).
4. Be willing to suffer wrong.
   - "To have lawsuits at all with one another is already a defeat for you. Why not rather suffer wrong? Why not rather be defrauded?" (1 Corinthians 6:7).

Applying these passages requires powerful commitment.

Peter writes, "Likewise, husbands, live with your wives in an understanding way, showing honor to the woman as the weaker vessel, since they are heirs with you of the grace of life, so that your prayers may not be hindered" (1 Peter 3:7). This feels particularly hard when she has something against you or when she has sinned against you. But remember, seeking reconciliation is doing her good; it's how you protect your marriage and your prayer life.

Following Jesus' Command

The ministry of Jesus focuses on reconciliation. His purpose for coming to earth centered on reconciling us to God. If we're doing the work of Jesus, we have to be focused on reconciliation too. In the

Sermon on the Mount, Jesus teaches about the reconciliation requirement for all believers:

> "If you are offering your gift at the altar and there remember that your brother has something against you, leave your gift there before the altar and go. First be reconciled to your brother, and then come and offer your gift."
>
> MATTHEW 5:23-24

Does your wife have something against you? Jesus says "something"—not "a big thing," not "a sin thing," not "a provable thing"—just *something*. The Greek word used is an indefinite pronoun and can be translated "something" or "anything." And He doesn't say, "if it's legitimate" or "if it's causing you problems." You're commanded by Jesus to seek reconciliation immediately, even if you're mid-worship.

Later in Matthew, Jesus makes a statement that's different in almost every way: "If your brother sins against you, go and tell him his fault, between you and him alone. If he listens to you, you have gained your brother" (Matthew 18:15). Nothing ambiguous here. In this case, it's not about something or anything that could be nothing; this is about sin. If your brother has sinned against you, it's a very different stipulation. You're again told to go seek reconciliation in a specific way—privately between just the two of you.

In both cases, Jesus tells *you* to do it. Does your wife have anything against you? You go seek reconciliation. Has she sinned against you? You go seek reconciliation.

Both passages focus on doing what it takes to be reconciled. Reconciliation happens when

- whoever is being sinful (which is often both people) repents,
- at least one of you humbles yourself and serves the other's best interest at personal cost, and
- you assign grace to the other person out of the overflow of the grace Jesus has bought for you.

This is a time-demanding process. It requires intentional, sacrificial action.

Sometimes, though, one-to-one reconciliation doesn't work. What then?

In the same passage in which He commands us to seek reconciliation, Jesus points out that reconciliation may require several different, escalating steps. And even then, sometimes it doesn't work: "If your brother sins against you, go and tell him his fault, between you and him alone. If he listens to you, you have gained your brother. But if he does not listen, take one or two others along with you, that every charge may be established by the evidence of two or three witnesses. If he refuses to listen to them, tell it to the church. And if he refuses to listen even to the church, let him be to you as a Gentile and a tax collector" (Matthew 18:15-17).

Notice that we don't have the option to just walk away after attempting reconciliation when the situation involves sin. If the private approach doesn't work, we're told to take one or two other people with us to speak with the person, again to continue seeking reconciliation. If the "charge" is established by the evidence of two or three people but the person isn't swayed, then we're to take it to the church. If that step doesn't result in repentance, the next step is to distance ourselves from the person—to break fellowship with the goal of him or her realizing the seriousness and loss enough to want to be reconciled.

More often than not, especially in marriage, we refuse to obey Jesus in this. Instead, we harbor complaints against our spouses without taking the first step toward reconciliation. We pull others into gossip and slander, to venting and maligning, without even the ruse of seeking reconciliation. We refuse to take the issue "to the church," but we take it *from* the church by harboring resentment, by growing cold and leaving the matter unresolved.

We often try to make the issue about our spouses. However, James points out that we're to look intently in the Word to see ourselves: "If anyone is a hearer of the word and not a doer, he is like a man who looks intently at his natural face in a mirror. For he looks at himself and goes away and at once forgets what he was like. But the one who looks into the perfect law, the law of liberty, and perseveres, being no hearer who forgets but a doer who acts, he will be blessed in his doing" (James 1:23-25).

> **Pursuing reconciliation is a personal responsibility. Pursuing reconciliation is your personal responsibility.**

The Word is a mirror, designed for each son of God to look at himself in it and be changed. Far too often, we treat the Word the way a parent uses the rearview mirror in the car to keep an eye on a kid in a car seat—we direct the mirror away from us and point it at the other person. We focus on our spouse, and our spouse focuses on us. Sadly, no one sees him- or herself, and no one changes. Look intently at this mirror with the focus on yourself. Be a doer who acts, and be blessed in the doing.

Countdown Journal

How will focusing on reconciliation help you fight well?

How will you remind yourself that the goal is reconciling, not winning?

Anniversary Reflection

What part of reconciliation is the most difficult?

DAY 10

Invest Wisely, Steward Intentionally

Mike and I were finally being consistent in reading the Bible together, and we were working our way through the Old Testament. When we read Haggai 1:6, "He who earns wages does so to put them into a bag with holes," we both felt like it was describing us.

That passage describes a lot of people. A 2024 Ramsey Solutions study shows that nearly half of Americans struggled paying their bills.[1] We've certainly walked in those shoes. From the time we got married, we've both worked. We've lived like most Americans—a very blessed lifestyle compared to much of the world. We weren't going hungry by any means. But during most of the early years, we lived paycheck to paycheck. I dreaded the grocery store checkout. Our credit cards always seemed stretched. We had next to no savings. Many of our arguments were triggered by financial strain.

Over several weeks, that verse kept coming to mind as our Bible reading took us through Haggai and Zechariah and into Malachi. Then one morning, as Mike read aloud Malachi 3:10, I vividly remember being struck by the dichotomy between it and the Haggai verse. Malachi 3:10 says, "Bring the full tithe into the storehouse, that there may be food in my house. And thereby put me to the test, says the Lord of hosts, if I will not open the windows of heaven for you and pour down for you a blessing until there is no more need."

We had holes in our pockets. It felt as if the money ran out of our accounts as fast as or faster than it went in, and we had little influence on the inflow. We were both salaried, so no matter how much we worked, our pay was the same. The pay wasn't bad, but it was fixed, and we didn't see much likelihood it would change anytime soon. Haggai 1 felt like our reality, and Malachi 3 seemed like a dream.

We dug into that passage in our discussion. We got a little hung up on the word *tithe*. In short, it refers to a tenth, and the Old Testament laws include three distinctive tithes. However, most biblical scholars agree that the Old Testament principle of giving a tenth of your income—usually flocks and crops in that agrarian society—is not taught as a New Testament principle. They agree that lessons can be garnered through a study of tithing but that Jesus' teachings and the other New Testament writings focus on giving regularly, intentionally, joyfully, and sacrificially when necessary.

When Mike and I read Malachi 3 together, we asked ourselves, "If we really believe that God will open the heavens and pour down blessings until there is no more need if we give the whole tithe . . . what should we do?" We had to acknowledge that we'd always discussed our Christmas and vacation plans and budget—even our plans for date nights—more thoroughly than we'd ever addressed our giving.

We talked about the profound difference. We found joy in spending on Christmas gifts for each other and others. We looked forward to vacations and were more than happy to save for them, even if it required sacrifice. If we didn't agree about how much to spend on these kinds of things, it was worth it to both of us to work through the conflict. Really, our approach to setting aside money for Christmas, vacations, and dates lined up more with Jesus and the New Testament writers than our offerings ever had.

Now, however, we agreed that because *we really believed* Malachi 3:10 and Jesus' guidance on giving, we needed to review our finances and adjust them to give our whole offering in a way that honored Jesus and our commitment to be like Him.

Now we review our finances annually and throughout the year, investing time and energy to be sure we're giving the whole tithe to God's work. That means that we give an agreed-upon amount that corresponds with what He's giving to us, that we plan and prepare to give with excited expectation (like with Christmas and vacations), and that we stick to the plan even when it requires some sacrifice.

The Meaning of *Stewardship*

If you say the word *invest* or *steward* to people, money is the primary—if not the only—thing that comes to mind. Money is going to be a problem in your life and in your marriage at many points. Learning to invest and steward money wisely will help you avoid some of the most difficult times, but money will still be troublesome. If you can learn to invest and steward all God has given you, money will become less troublesome, because you will come to focus on it less. God's gifts and generous outpouring will become ever more your focus. God has given you time, talents, and abilities. Being a good steward and investing wisely are principles that should guide your use of all these gifts.

Some simple and specific verses spell out God's fundamental truths about money:

- *Do not love money or become greedy.* Paul warned Timothy and warns us that "the love of money is a root of all kinds of evils. It is through this craving that some have wandered away from the faith and pierced themselves with many pangs" (1 Timothy 6:10). In Hebrews 13:5, Scripture says, "Keep your life free from love of money, and be content with what you have, for he has said, 'I will never leave you nor forsake you.'"
- *Pay what you owe and avoid borrowing money.* Romans 13:7-8 sums it up like this: "Pay to all what is owed to them: taxes

to whom taxes are owed, revenue to whom revenue is owed, respect to whom respect is owed, honor to whom honor is owed. Owe no one anything, except to love each other, for the one who loves another has fulfilled the law." You will likely have a mortgage and occasionally borrow money, but try not to borrow unless the investment or outcome outweighs the risk and interest. The goal is to become debt-free and able to help others generously.

- *When you can help people who are poor or your family, do not charge interest.* I'm not indicting banks, finance companies, or business investments. This principle is a personal charge about individuals lending to individuals, and it's straight from Scripture: "If you lend money to any of my people with you who is poor, you shall not be like a moneylender to him, and you shall not exact interest from him" (Exodus 22:25). Another passage, Deuteronomy 23:19, commands, "You shall not charge interest on loans to your brother, interest on money, interest on food, interest on anything that is lent for interest."

  Don't stretch this out of context. Mike has been in the banking industry his entire career, and banks are built on providing loans for interest. Car dealerships and mortgage companies all rely on interest fees to generate revenue. This first passage talks about us personally helping people who are poor and about how we should not charge interest when we lend to them.

  The second passage talks about not charging a brother interest. Mike and I have at times been able to help others. We've agreed that our first responsibilities are our tithe and providing for our family. We don't give money or buy anything that jeopardizes our tithe or providing for our children. Our second commitment has been to never give or lend what we can't afford to lose, and as often as we can, we prefer to give rather than lend. The rare times when we've felt compelled to personally lend rather than give, we haven't charged interest.

This premise appears as both a literal command and, in the Matthew 18 parable of the servant who owes ten thousand talents, an allegorical lesson about forgiving all kinds of debts because we've been forgiven of much more. You remember the story: The servant begs to be forgiven a huge debt, equivalent to approximately two hundred thousand years, or *seventy-three million days*, of labor.[2] The master feels pity for the servant and forgives the debt completely.

We're called as individuals to help people in need, and we're called to do it without expecting any gain.

Forgiven and debt-free, the servant goes out and brutally attacks another servant over a debt of only one hundred days of labor. The master, when he hears of the hateful attack, reinstates the debt and has the servant thrown in jail "until he should pay the debt" (Matthew 18:30). Think that through—until he paid off seventy-three million days of labor. Jesus ends the story with a sobering statement: "So also my heavenly Father will do to every one of you, if you do not forgive your brother from your heart" (Matthew 18:35).

- *Grow what God gives you through work or business.* As you've been reading this, you may have thought about Matthew 25 and the parable of the talents given to the three servants. Don't get confused by the "don't charge interest" command when it comes to benevolence and the expectation of return on investment in the parable of the talents. The parable of the talents has nothing to do with benevolence; it's about stewardship, employment, and business.

  This parable clearly reveals that whatever we've received from God we've received as an endowment from Him to do His work. As powerful as that lesson is, the layers of the parable reveal even more—and the part we often miss is the reassuring truth that God Himself equips us to do the work He asks of us.

It's easy to miss a phrase in verse 15 that explains the difference in what the three servants are given: The master gives "to each according to his ability." The Greek word translated "ability" can refer to power, might, or strength,[3] and in the New Testament it's often associated with the use of miraculous power.

Do you see that? Really absorb it. The master gives the talent(s) to each servant that that servant has the strength, might, and perhaps even miraculous power to manage.

The one-talent servant receives the talent he has the strength, might, and perhaps even miraculous power to manage. The five-talent servant likewise receives the talents he has the strength, might, and perhaps even miraculous power to manage.

One silver or gold talent is estimated to weigh seventy-five to one hundred pounds.[4] These are heavy amounts of precious metals. But the master expects each servant to use his personal talent(s) to invest and grow these sums according to his abilities.

You have so much because God has given you so much—a mind and body that grow in strength, a woman you love, the ability to work and earn money, and most of all, salvation through Jesus.

> **God has given you talents that may feel heavy, but He's given you the abilities to invest and grow them. He expects you to invest them for His glory!**

Those talents will sometimes be quite heavy in your life. Don't let fear and self-reliance weigh you down or cripple you the way they do the one-talent servant. Trust that the God of the universe, your Abba (Father), has fully equipped you to invest and steward all He has given you. Don't hoard what He's entrusted to you. Celebrate the journey, lead the way, invest, and steward your talents (including money—but also much more) for His glory.

- *Honor God with the full tithe, sewing up the holes in your finances.* I wish I had started reading Scripture and really challenging my deep beliefs and commitments much sooner. But in virtually every biblical study and every reading of Scripture we do, Mike and I now use this two-phrase review:

 The assessment: "If I really believed ___________, then ___________."
 The commitment: "Because I really believe ___________, then ___________."

God's promises do not return empty (see Isaiah 55:11). He's faithful. So return to Him joyfully a share of your finances and your time. We've found that it's impossible to outgive Him. Our obedience in our giving has built our faith as we've walked together in stewarding and returning a small part of all He gives us. Sew up the holes in your pockets sooner than we did!

Countdown Journal

What are some of the talents God has given you?

What are some of the talents God has given your fiancée?

What are some of the talents God has given you both as a couple?

Anniversary Reflection

What's the evidence that you're stewarding God's gifts well?

What talents are you hiding or holding back?

Are there any signs you're trusting gifts rather than God?

DAY 9

Love Her as Christ Loves the Church

Mike enjoys a good steak. He likes eating one; he likes cooking one. Few things make him happier than a Friday night spent on our back porch watching a bit of football while a steak sizzles on his grill. He looks forward to those nights. He plans for them. He goes to a specific store, not our usual grocery store, to get the right steak. He doesn't even complain about cleaning up the kitchen after a good steak dinner.

What's something you enjoy like that? Something you look forward to, something you plan for and you're not just willing but eager to make special effort for? We all have something like Mike's steak nights. We might even say we *love* it.

We tend to toss that word around liberally. "I love a hot bath." "I love chocolate." "I love reading." So when we say, "I love you," it can be unclear exactly what we mean and how much we mean it. But in His wisdom, God doesn't leave the definition vague when He tells husbands to love their wives.

A Biblical View

Ephesians 5 gives a clear standard for the love a husband should have for his wife. Nearing the end of the chapter, Paul writes, "In the same way husbands should love their wives as their own bodies. He who loves his wife loves himself. For no one ever hated his own flesh, but nourishes and cherishes it, just as Christ does the church, because we are members of his body" (Ephesians 5:28-30).

Far too often we read verses like that and want to hold the beauty of the image without taking hold of the application. But Paul has a much clearer view of what walking in love and giving oneself up for another means. In our superficial culture, we toss the word *love* around loosely. We think of flowers and hearts.

For Paul, however, the passion Christ has for the church doesn't elicit images of rose petals and candlelight. It generates images of sacrifice and hard work, long days and long journeys. The fragrant offering and sacrifice of Christ came through torture and anguish, culminating in His death. Paul has witnessed crucifixions. He has experienced meeting the resurrected Savior on the road to Damascus. Jesus' love for us required that He leave the Father and His rightful place in heaven to live a difficult life on earth as a man.

In the last third of Ephesians 5, Paul focuses on the specific challenges of walking out the love of Jesus in marriage. Repeatedly Paul points out that the love of Christ is submissive and sacrificial. We don't like those words; the world around us despises them.

> **In every respect, Scripture commands you to be understanding toward your wife, show her honor, and love her as Jesus does.**

Christ's commitment to His bride caused Him to leave His earthly mother to minister to broken and hurting people. For His bride, He suffered unjust treatment, betrayal, and torture in her place. For the one who had sinned and broken the laws requiring punishment, Jesus assumed the debt; He faced the judgment. For the church, Jesus was beaten and broken. For her betrayal—*her betrayal of Him*—He was tried, sentenced, and punished. For His bride, He pursued her, fought for her, suffered for her, stepped into guilt's path for her.

You, likewise, are called to love your wife so much that you're willing to lay down your life for her. She's precious. The apostle Peter refers to her as "the weaker vessel": "Likewise, husbands, live with your wives in an understanding way, showing honor to the woman as the weaker vessel, since they are heirs with you of the grace of life, so that your prayers may not be hindered" (1 Peter 3:7).

Don't get caught up in that single thought and lose sight of the powerful message in this verse. The point is not to minimize women. We all know women are often strong and powerful; we know men can be weak or frail.

The key idea of the verse is the role you're supposed to take in relationship to her; it's not a controversial commentary on her status or capacity. Focus on the message to you and to all husbands: She's a joint heir, a child of God. Be strong for her. This is so important, the verse says, that failure to treat your wife with understanding and honor *will hinder your prayers.*

Reread that incredible, culture-confronting statement on the elevation of women, countercultural both in the time and culture in which it was originally written and today. Peter wrote it when women had little to no standing in the community in a culture where inheritance was strictly a right of males and a woman's status legally was less than that of a male child. The instruction to Christian husbands was to treat women with understanding and honor because Jesus had made them *equal heirs of grace!*

Look around at our modern culture, which espouses equality but—hypocritically—denigrates women in movies and advertising. One in three women across the world experiences violence;[1] one in ten girls worldwide experiences sexual violence at some point in her life;[2] of all women killed globally in 2012, it's estimated that almost 50 percent were killed by a partner or relative (compared to less than 6 percent of men killed);[3] and more than 230 million girls and women alive have undergone female genital mutilation.[4]

Scripture clearly condemns harm to women, but it doesn't stop at just saying, "Don't mistreat your wife." The Bible calls you to love her as yourself. According to Paul, she is to you as your own body (Ephesians 5:28). He goes on to make this practical, saying that no man hates his own body—he feeds and protects it, nourishes and cherishes it, just as Jesus nourishes and cherishes His body, the church (Ephesians 5:29-30).

Loving Your Wife

Look back at all the ways Jesus fed and protected people during His earthly life: filling once-empty fishing nets, turning water to wine, feeding thousands with a child's lunch, washing feet on the night of His last supper, being unafraid to touch someone with leprosy, restoring sight, raising the dead, forgiving His torturers, and paying our debts with His life and blood. His love and nurture were lavish and abundant. Jesus calls you to nurture your wife, to cherish her, and to protect her like that.

> **Love your wife with more passion than any other earthly pursuit!**

When our older son, Patrick, wanted to learn to play guitar, he studied books on music and practiced until his fingertips were raw. He sought out lessons. He built his own pedalboard. When our younger son, Colten, started playing soccer, he chased that ball all over the yard. He listened to the coaches. He ran drills that helped him play better with a team.

When both of them decided to become healthier and stronger, they completely changed their lifestyles. Eating became intentional and sacrificial. They got up early, tired or not, and battled through the heat and the cold to work out. They spent hard-earned money on the tools and equipment that would help them get stronger. They learned from mentors, men who had been doing it longer, men who were stronger. Perhaps you've done similar things in pursuit of some passion.

Love your wife like that, but even more and for the rest of your

Change your lifestyle completely from one of singleness to one of unity—unity with God and unity with your wife.

life. Chase her. Watch her with enthusiasm. Find a marriage coach and listen to them. Run the marriage drills (taking out the trash, picking up your dirty underwear, loading the dishwasher) that will help you be a better teammate. Meet the opponent (who wants to destroy your marriage) head-on using all the armor of God. Go on a lifelong quest to get better as a husband, to improve your strengths, to overcome weaknesses, to encourage her, to be the leader she needs.

It's Not Easy

I'm not saying this is easy, especially if there are grievances. I've found that repentance, reconciliation, and forgiveness are rarely one and done. Repentance often requires several steps and sometimes multiple attempts. Reconciliation almost always requires time and multiple actions. Forgiveness is often an ongoing process. Over the years since Mike and I together made the commitment to stay married and do the hard work of reconciliation, we've had to recommit time and time again.

Be intentional and sacrificial in your marriage. Give up self-indulgence. Get up early, tired or not, to spend time with your wife and help her. Battle through the heat of arguments and her cold shoulder to get better. Give up time watching television and playing games. Spend hard-earned money on tools and equipment to help you. Learn from mentors, men who have been married longer, men whose marriages are stronger.

In Mark 12, when a scribe asks, "Which commandment is the most important of all?" Jesus says, "The most important is, 'Hear, O Israel: The Lord our God, the Lord is one. And you shall love the Lord your God with all your heart and with all your soul and with all your mind and with all your strength.' The second is this: 'You shall love your neighbor as yourself.' There is no other commandment greater than these" (Mark 12:28-31).

If you love God with all your heart (passion), soul (life), mind (intellect), and strength (body) and love your neighbor as yourself, you'll be more than willing and eager to spend time with the One and the ones you love. You'll want to grow closer to them.

You'll learn to speak your wife's love language. You'll let go of the pride and self-protection that lead to criticism, contempt, defensiveness, and stonewalling. You'll pursue the best for the One and the one you love. Jesus says that "on these two commandments depend all the Law and the Prophets" (Matthew 22:40). Amen. On these two commands hang every good piece of marital advice: Love God and love your neighbor.

Soon your fiancée will be your wife and nearest neighbor—just across the bed.

Love her as yourself.

Countdown Journal

How will your bride feel if you love her as Christ loves the church, if you're willing not only to die for her but also to live for her?

What will you be willing to do to live for her—genuinely and daily?

Anniversary Reflection

What scores have been kept that need to be erased? What forgiveness do you need to extend?

DAY 8

Rejoice! (Step 1 for Fighting Well)

When Mike and I got married, we believed in Jesus. We both had chosen Him as Lord of our lives, our first and last. We were young and had a lot of maturing to do, but we had committed to Him as our cornerstone. What we weren't, however, was intentional in studying how to be married according to God and applying Scripture to every aspect of our relationship.

We were decades into our marriage when we found ourselves in a difficult, ongoing argument. The kind that's the evidence of a brewing, unresolved, serious issue. The kind that weaves itself around and through daily activities because it continues unresolved while jobs and housework and church demand your attention.

An argument that breeds contempt and resentment allows the enemy to gain a stronghold in a marriage.

One of us had sinned—me. I had lost my temper and been unkind and disrespectful. Both of us were angry and hurt. Neither of us could get past it. We were barely speaking to each other, and when we did speak, the words were sharp and loaded.

We were at a conference together, and we had just walked away from each other, angry and frustrated. Mike went to his next session; I stormed off to find a place to stew. I like to believe it was an attempt to calm myself that led me to walk away, find a quiet spot, and open my Bible on my phone. If I'm painfully honest, however, it was more likely an attempt to make myself feel more spiritual and less guilty.

A Life-Changing Discovery

I found a quiet table by a fountain. I started reading in 2 Corinthians 13, and it felt as if Paul were speaking directly to me about our fight. I don't know if you have conversations with yourself like I do. On that occasion, it was that discussion in my head that opened my eyes to a pattern for fighting well written by Paul.

If any of the New Testament writers had the clout to address how to fight a good fight, it would have to be Paul. After all, the Holy Spirit used him to coin the phrase *I have fought the good fight* (2 Timothy 4:7). Throughout his life after his conversion and in all his writing, Paul encouraged and taught and emphasized the importance of love and unity, but he never hid from a good fight.

For example, Paul confronted Peter face-to-face (see Galatians 2:11-14). Challenged within the church and without, he stood his ground for the truth. His letters all reflect his willingness to fight well. In the letters to the Corinthians, Paul teaches us how to deal with conflict, with sin, and with church discipline.

So I began to read 2 Corinthians 13. Now, I confess that for years I had read Scripture in the way many people often do—a quick and cursory reading to gather a surface-level understanding and a superficial application to Christians as a group. I would read a passage. The words would make sense. I'd think, *Yep, we Christians should do that, and man, my life would be better if all the other Christians would really do this, especially the ones closest to me, like my spouse, my kids, and my siblings.*

This time, however, I decided to slow down, read intentionally, carefully listen, deeply examine my heart and actions against the truth, and do what Scripture said—even and especially when it felt awkward.

It's hard to explain how the passage affected me. But what I discovered in that passage that day—what I'm convinced the Holy Spirit shared with me—changed our lives (specifically the way we resolve conflicts) forever.

As I read through the chapter, I realized God was speaking to *me*. *I* was at fault; *I* needed to examine myself; *I* needed to look in the mirror of God's Word and change. *We* (Mike and I) needed to build up and restore our relationship, not continue to damage it. But how?

And then I came to verses 11-12:

> Finally, brothers, rejoice. Aim for restoration, comfort one another, agree with one another, live in peace; and the God of love and peace will be with you. Greet one another with a holy kiss.
>
> 2 CORINTHIANS 13:11-12

Suddenly I saw it: six imperative verbs—*five steps for fighting well, for getting to restoration, and a celebration at the end.* On this day and the five that follow, we'll explore those verbs in detail.

The First Step

So I opened my eyes and looked at each imperative, starting with *rejoice*. The *Merriam-Webster Dictionary* defines *rejoice* as "feel joy or great delight."[1] In the Bible, rejoicing occurs at Jesus' birth, at the return of the prodigal son, at the one lost lamb's being returned to the ninety-nine in the fold, at the saving of a soul, and at the marriage supper of the Lamb. Picture each one of these scenes. How does rejoicing in each of these experiences look? Big smiles? Deep sighs of satisfaction? Outbursts of joy? Laughter?

By definition, then, step 1 is to feel great joy or delight with each other. Go have some delight. Whatever you need to do, find a way to smile and laugh and share cheerfulness. This isn't a whimsical or flippant suggestion. Repeatedly in Scripture, and in this specific sequence of steps, it's an imperative, an order, a command. What love the Father has for us—to command us to go have some fun, to feel joy!

When you're feeling the rumblings of a disagreement, find a way to rejoice together. Call a time-out and watch a video that makes you laugh or play a game you both enjoy. Eat a treat that makes you sigh with pleasure. Or, as a married couple, go make out for a while. As soon as the disagreement threatens, before cross words have had a chance to start or to continue, before you work through the necessary argument—stop and rejoice together. If you're doing this intentionally and as an act of obedience, it will feel awkward. Do it anyway.

We did just that during that argument at the conference, the one that had been replaying in our marriage for quite some time. When Mike came out of his meeting, he found me. I took a deep breath and said, "I think we should pause the argument and go have some fun."

His look was a bit confused, a lot relieved.

We called a truce and went to find a nice place for dinner. After the hostess seated us, we sat silent for a couple of minutes. We couldn't help but laugh about how awkward it felt to hit pause on an argument and decide to have fun. It was new to us, and we weren't even sure how to do it. We pushed through, though, and dinner really turned into a fun evening.

Paul didn't just command rejoicing—even when life is hard—he lived it out. In prison, Paul sang. Under persecution, he counted his blessings. During suffering, he rejoiced: "I rejoice in my sufferings for your sake, and in my flesh I am filling up what is lacking in Christ's afflictions for the sake of his body, that is, the church" (Colossians 1:24).

Awkward to sing in prison? Surely. Difficult to be cheerful while being persecuted? No doubt. An act of intentional obedience to rejoice in suffering? Absolutely. But if Paul could sing in prison and rejoice in suffering, we can call a time-out before we do the hard work of a good fight to acknowledge the blessings, to have some fun, and to celebrate life, including and especially with this person God has joined to you in marriage.

Countdown Journal

What brings easy laughter and joy to you as a couple?

List three ways you can step away from a disagreement and bring joy to your fiancée first—before you address the issue.

Anniversary Reflection

How have you rejoiced together before heavy conversations?

What do you need to do differently so you can rejoice more easily?

DAY 7

Aim for Restoration (Step 2 for Fighting Well)

Jesus has promised that we have the power to do much more than we think. I remember the day Mike and I read Matthew 21 together in our morning devotions. We were both touched by the interaction Jesus had with the fig tree and the lesson He taught about our ability to do what He calls us to do.

Mike and I had read the story before, probably several times, perhaps missing the impact because our attention had fallen to the powerful events around it. Jesus has just entered Jerusalem like a triumphant king riding on a colt, fulfilling prophecy and fanning the embers that will cause the religious leaders to burn with rage. Then Jesus clears the Temple, driving out money-changers with a whip as He declares, "'My house shall be called a house of prayer,' but you make it a den of robbers" (Matthew 21:13).

Then, almost lost against those larger-than-life, loud and powerful visual images of Jesus, Matthew tells what seems at first to be just a casual story, almost a space filler. The next day, Jesus is hungry as he enters Bethany. He walks up to a fig tree, hoping He will find some figs even though they're out of season. Finding none, however, He curses the tree: "May no fruit ever come from you again!" (Matthew 21:19).

The day we read that story, I laughed as it struck me that even Jesus, it appeared, could get "hangry." Mike tries to keep me from going too long without eating because we both know hunger makes me irritable. The story stuck with both of us. I wrote "Stupid Fig Tree" in the margin of my Bible.

Amid our joking, we almost missed the following passage. But it grabbed us:

> Jesus answered them, "Truly, I say to you, if you have faith and do not doubt, you will not only do what has been done to the fig tree, but even if you say to this mountain, 'Be taken up and thrown into the sea,' it will happen. And whatever you ask in prayer, you will receive, if you have faith."
>
> MATTHEW 21:21-22

Whoa! We had to sit with that for a minute. Here we were struggling with some little molehills of unresolved issues we just kept putting off. We were trying to avoid them at worst and work around them at best—faltering at both. But Jesus told us we could tell mountains to move. Could we really just speak to them and they would be removed? Could we curse the stupid fig tree and let it never bear fruit again? That conversation opened our eyes to the possibility of restoration and the importance of dealing with things directly, of "speaking to them" and taking a stand.

Identifying the Bull's-Eye

As we've discussed, the first step in fighting well is to rejoice. If you didn't experience joy in step 1, go back and try again. It can be awkward, but it will *revolutionize* your fights.

The second step Paul lists is to aim for restoration. *Aim* means "to direct toward a specified object or goal."[1] Restoration is the act of restoring—renewal, revival, or reestablishment.

To help you make this an intentional step, get together with your wife and draw a target on a sheet of paper. (It can be just a circle inside a circle.) You can't aim for restoration if you don't know what has been or is being damaged, so in the center of the inner circle, each of you write a phrase or sentence that reveals what needs to be restored.

Don't write the problem or the argument; write what has been or is being damaged or threatened by the problem or disagreement. It may help to ask yourself, *If I lose this argument, what will be hurt or damaged, and how will I feel?*

For example, if you argue about how much money is being spent on a gym membership, the disagreement is likely that one person thinks the amount is justifiable and the other thinks it's too much. To decide what's in the bull's-eye, ask yourself, *If this ends up meaning that I can't keep spending that amount on the gym, what will be lost, and how will I feel?*

The answer may be that you won't be able to keep going to the gym, and that may make you feel as if fitness and other things that matter to you aren't important to her. It may make you feel insecure about how much money you make.

On the flip side, ask yourself, *If this ends up meaning that we keep spending money on the gym, what will be lost, and how will* she *feel?* She may feel that the membership is too expensive and will prevent you from being able to pay for household needs or other things she prioritizes. She may feel like you're choosing yourself over her.

Whatever has been or is being damaged by the disagreement and whatever would be or could be lost or hurt by this argument should be written in the bull's-eye.

Don't argue about the validity of what either of you writes there. If either of you feels that something is being threatened or has been damaged or has never been whole, restoration is needed. This part has little to do with how the argument will be settled and much to do with being obedient to Scripture and loving your wife with your actions.

This is about understanding and respecting her views. To do this step well, you need to disconnect whatever she writes in the circle from blame or justification.

Even if you completely disagree with what your wife writes, still don't discount or debate her feelings. You're still commanded to aim for restoration. Together you may earn plenty of money. If so, you need to work to restore her confidence, to help her feel secure with the level of your income.

If her feelings are rooted in reality, however, you must address those facts. For example, if there isn't enough money to keep paying for the gym membership, you must change. You can't restore something that will continue to be damaged or broken. It's a waste of time, like bailing water from a sinking boat without plugging the hole in the bottom. In that case, you must cut back on going to the gym, use another means of exercise, or find a way to make more money.

> Her feelings are her feelings. Even if the argument or the situation doesn't justify those feelings, she does feel them. You must start by understanding and accepting her feelings.

Your job is to restore whatever has been damaged or is at risk. If your wife is worrying about money, you can't just say, "Don't worry about it." You should discover what's frustrating her and what helps her feel confident. You have to be her partner and the one who works to restore whatever she's listed in the bull's-eye. If she needs $6,750 in the savings account to be able to feel okay about paying for the gym membership, then you work toward that goal together.

Jesus Our Example

Jesus is the ultimate restorer—in little matters like being hungry or tired and in the biggest of issues, our separation from God.

Jesus doesn't just aim for restoration—He accomplishes it. Smiling at His mother's needling at a wedding, He restored wine to empty party glasses. When the multitude felt tired and hungry and the disciples felt overwhelmed by their needs, Jesus restored both with a few loaves and fish. As the storm raged and the disciples felt fear and panic, Jesus restored their sense of security by calming the storm. After Peter stepped out of the boat boldly but then fearfully began to sink, Jesus lifted him up. Weeping with Mary and Martha, Jesus restored Lazarus to life and to his sisters.

Jesus alone can complete restoration, but we're often the tools He uses.

Jesus restored us to relationship with Him through humility and sacrifice. We're called to be like Him. By humbling ourselves and serving like Him, we can aim for and find restoration. We can curse what should never be allowed to bear fruit in our lives again! Whatever it is, then, that your spouse or my spouse does, whatever it is that you or I do, Jesus has more than covered that issue with His blood. Restoration is possible; with faith it is promised.

Countdown Journal

What's the difference between aiming for restoration and trying to change your fiancée's feelings?

How will you stay focused on reconciling rather than proving your point?

Anniversary Reflection

What issue has come up repeatedly over the past year?

What are the feelings, fears, hurts, or losses at the heart of the issue that you need your wife to restore or that she needs you to restore?

DAY 6

Comfort Each Other (Step 3 for Fighting Well)

Our extended family had a tough run of illness and death when both our sons were in college. My mom's Alzheimer's disease advanced to the point where she needed full-time care. Quite unexpectedly, my dad, who had always seemed like a powerhouse of energy, became ill. As the New Year arrived, he was diagnosed with stage 4 pancreatic cancer. He died five months later.

Then one day, Mike's dad, Charles, called from Arkansas because he was being hospitalized with pneumonia. We jumped in the car and started the five-hour drive to visit and help him get back on his feet. We both thought it would be a couple of days away from home. We had been there only a couple of hours when it became obvious that this trip was not just a visit but would require us to move Charles home with us.

Mike's dad was determined he was going to his own home. Mike was overwhelmed by the sudden downturn in his dad's health, the unexpected turn of events, and the awareness of what lay ahead since he had had a front row seat to the decline of my parents. The brewing fight between the two men was tough to witness.

Mike's dad was in almost full denial of the severity of his illness.

We quickly learned what he had wasn't just pneumonia but double pneumonia. Then we found he had been diagnosed, without telling Mike and maybe not fully understanding himself, with pulmonary fibrosis, which we soon discovered was end-stage.

The fight stirred, but Mike knew this was not a fight *with* his dad but *for* his dad. Charles couldn't go home. But rather than push his dad to accept that he would have to live with us, Mike offered it as a visit, a chance to see his grandsons and spend some time with Mike as Charles recovered. Rather than push Mike to figure it all out or try to come up with solutions, I focused on helping him find ways to rejoice with Charles during his "visit."

As each challenge appeared, we focused on identifying what was making Charles resist help and tried to restore whatever he felt he was losing—which was mostly his independence. At a time when arguments escalated easily, the Holy Spirit gave us both the peace of mind to comfort Charles and each other.

We couldn't do a single thing to stop the progression of Charles's illness, but we could enjoy every minute of time we had with him. So we got him set up to watch baseball games with his son and grandsons. We made sure he had food he could enjoy. We sought hospice care to help us. We comforted him for quite a while before we addressed coming to agreement on next steps.

The Third Step

This third step of comforting each other should only be tried after intentionally completing the first two: rejoicing and restoring. Those take the power and sting away from the enemy and remind you and your wife that you're on the same side. You're declaring the truth of Ephesians 6:12—*your battle is not with flesh and blood.*

The disagreement you're facing, no matter how large or small, has its root in the fall and is being spurred on and celebrated by the enemy. If you're making plans for a great mission trip to share the gospel and a silly argument over a minor point arises, the argument is the strategy of the enemy trying to encroach on your shared ministry. If the frustration is over what you'll have for dinner, the enemy is planting a seed.

The New Testament Greek verb for "comfort" is *parakaleō*. It is formed from *para*, a preposition indicating close proximity, and *kaleō*, which means "to call."[1] It communicates the idea of calling one another near. The first two steps break down the barriers the enemy tries to build between you and your wife so you can come near to each other in the third.

> You cannot comfort someone else, especially someone with whom you're arguing, unless you intentionally channel the comfort of the Father.

In 2 Corinthians 1:3-4, Paul praises God for being our comforter and for enabling us to comfort others: "Blessed be the God and Father of our Lord Jesus Christ, the Father of mercies and God of all comfort, who comforts us in all our affliction, so that we may be able to comfort those who are in any affliction, with the comfort with which we ourselves are comforted by God."

Every use of the word *comfort* in the verses above is *parakaleo* or the related noun *paraklēsis*. If we replace the word *comfort* with the meaning "call [another] near," listen to the message:

> Blessed be the God and Father of our Lord Jesus Christ, the Father of mercies and God of all efforts to call us near, who calls us near in all our affliction, so that we may be able to call near those who are in any affliction, with the same effort of calling near with which we ourselves have been called near by God.

We can comfort others because God comforts us when we're distressed. He's the model for how you're to comfort your wife. He cleared the path for us to come near to Him even while we were yet sinners (see Romans 5:8). He calls us near when we're troubled. He saves us and comforts us even—especially—in our weakness.

Jesus fought to win the victory over death for us; the eternal God made Himself mortal to make us immortal.

Scripture gives us the example of Jesus exercising each of these steps of fighting well in the greatest and most beautiful fight. *The only good fight is a fight in which you're fighting for the other person as well as, or even instead of, yourself.* Jesus certainly fought for us.

Jesus' Example

Remember that in 2 Corinthians 13:11 the first step is to rejoice, *and Jesus came rejoicing.* He did what He did "for the joy that was set before him" (Hebrews 12:2). He exemplified a joyful life—caring for family; building deep friendships; sharing meals with people; working together with others; making people's lives better; and loving, crying, and laughing with others. His first miracle was at a place of rejoicing—a wedding!

He also exemplifies the second step: *Aim for restoration.* His entire thirty-three years on earth—and *all eternity—culminated at Golgotha for our restoration.*

Jesus moved right into step 3. Immediately after His resurrection, *He began comforting others even while the holes in His body created by stakes and spears gaped raw and open.* He comforted Mary at the tomb, turning tears of sorrow to joy by simply speaking her name. He appeared to the disciples cowering behind locked doors, turning fear into gladness as He showed them His hands and side. He returned another time to comfort Thomas, turning doubt into faith.

I love the story in John 21 of Jesus comforting seven of His disciples, once again powerfully exemplifying how to comfort another person—even when that person has been completely wrong and the one doing the comforting completely right.

Even after several interactions with the resurrected Savior, confusion and fear of the future seemed to be hanging over the disciples. Peter, it appears, decided he needed a break from the waiting and announced he was going fishing. Nathanael, James, John, Thomas, and two other disciples went along. The seven fished all night without catching anything.

At daybreak, someone hollered from the shoreline, "Children, do you have any fish?" (John 21:5).

I can imagine the aggravated, flat response: "No."

And, like generations of empty-handed fishermen, they received unsolicited advice: "Cast the net on the right side of the boat." I wonder if Peter heard the echo of a conversation three years earlier: "Put out into the deep and let down your nets for a catch." I wonder if he heard the echo of his own words: "Master, we toiled all night and took nothing! But at your word I will let down the nets" (Luke 5:4-5).

Jesus' disciples, His friends, had all fled, and Peter had denied Him as He had faced the hardest moment of His life, the eternally planned and eternity-altering act of restoring mankind to God through the cross.

I wonder if, when the net on the right side of the boat started to pull and sink from the load, Peter felt an overwhelming déjà vu. Peter's fishing partners, James and John, had also been with him three years earlier during another long night of fishing without success. I wonder if their hearts were beginning to beat faster as the recognition of the voice on the shoreline broke through their fatigue, as they realized it belonged to the One who had blessed them with the biggest catch of their entire careers just before calling them away to become fishers of men.

At that moment, Peter jumped into the water to swim to Jesus while the others dragged the net to the shore. When they arrived, fish still flopping, they found "a charcoal fire in place, with fish laid out on it, and bread" (John 21:9). Peter had not made amends with Jesus. Jesus hadn't pointed out the breach. That does happen later in the story, but not before He comforts him.

Stop for just a minute to really soak in this moment with Jesus. Imagine you're exhausted after trying unsuccessfully for long hours to do something you know how to do, something you've done your

Jesus didn't need their fish; He already had fish on the grill. But He still filled their nets to the breaking point, comforting them with success in a role they had known since childhood.

whole life. A friend shows up with a suggestion, and everything falls into place, better than you could have hoped for or have ever experienced. From frustration to triumph—the comfort of a helpful friend.

Then you turn around, and that same friend has a meal, hot and fresh, just about ready to hit your plate—the comfort of hot food when you're starving and satisfied with your work! But—and only a passionate fisherman, hunter, farmer, or cook might really understand this—your friend says, "Grab a few of those amazing fish you just caught [or *ducks you shot* or *homegrown tomatoes you harvested* or *pieces of that pie you baked*] and come eat with me." Every one of us needs the comfort of companionship—work and joy shared.

Comforting Your Wife

Often the little disagreements will end if you just take step 1. The fight may simply evaporate in your laughter. Some won't end as easily and will need step 2. If you listen to your wife's pain, fears, or frustration and then do whatever you can to restore what's hurt or damaged or at risk for her, you may very well resolve the fight right there. But when the damage is greater, you may find that step 3 is the point that brings the fight to an end.

I typically want to just jump over the first three steps. I can make all kinds of excuses for it: My upbringing. Mike's a big, strong guy, so he doesn't need all that. Mike isn't the touchy-feely type. We need to hurry. I'm too busy. And on and on. Thankfully, God helps me remember that Jesus never rushed.

I hope, of course, that life-and-death issues are way down the road for you. Maybe, for now, the restoration aim is to have that $6,750 in savings so your wife feels better about gym memberships or spending a bit extra on dates. It will take time to save money. Your next step doesn't have to wait for that. You can comfort her even while the savings account is stuck at $2,212.

If you go to her side, if you wrap your arms around her when she's staring at the savings-account statement, you may find that she takes a deep breath and her heart finds a calmer rhythm. You can comfort her by saying you've figured out a way to save fifty dollars a month on the phone bill and will put that in the savings account, getting you $600 closer over the next twelve months. You can comfort her—and call for powerful reinforcement—simply by making this one of your shared prayers: "Lord, You know we're working to get our savings up to $6,750, and I'm asking You to help us do that."

In any one of these steps, the fight may resolve. But when the core of the argument requires that you must change something to come into agreement with each other or that you must work together to find a way to agree, you'll need the fourth step—tomorrow's countdown message.

Countdown Journal

How will you model Jesus as you comfort your wife—even when you believe she's completely wrong?

What are the ways you encourage and comfort her now?

Anniversary Reflection

What has happened when you've let anger or frustration cause you to resist offering comfort to your wife?

What needs to change in your heart so that even when your wife is in the wrong you can still comfort and protect her as Jesus does?

DAY 5

Agree with Each Other (Step 4 for Fighting Well)

Imagine this scenario: Your wife is upset because a coworker said something that implied she wasn't doing her job. You don't think the coworker meant it the way she took it, and you think her feelings shouldn't be hurt. She thinks it was intentional, and you just don't understand.

You jump to step 4 in the process of fighting well—*seek agreement*—and begin trying to explain why her feelings shouldn't be hurt. The argument escalates.

You may not have to imagine it. Most of us have experienced this early and often in relationships. Laying it out as a scenario makes it obvious that seeking agreement in this kind of situation is going to lead to more hurt and a bigger fight.

Now imagine following the steps in 2 Corinthians 13:11-12 in that same situation. You see that your wife is hurt and know that one of the things that makes her happy is to take a walk with you. So you suggest a walk where she can tell you more about what happened. That's a small way to bring her joy. Then on the walk you encourage her to tell you what happened and how she was hurt by it. Just listen. Really listen. Ask questions only to make sure you understand. Let her talk.

Then imagine feeling how she feels—even if what happened wouldn't have made you feel that way. Voice your empathy. Try to reassure her of the truth about herself and to build her up, all as an effort to restore as much as you can of what has been damaged. Tell her how much you regret what's happening and how she feels. Comfort her the way God comforts us, the way you comfort friends.

A totally different outcome, right?

Steps in Order

Remember, no matter how natural it seems, don't move to step 4 until you have (1) rejoiced together, (2) set your aim for restoration, and (3) comforted each other. Don't start working to fix the disagreement, seeking agreement, until the fourth step. Too many small arguments, even just disappointments or rough days, turn into huge fights when we make the mistake of starting at step 4.

It may seem counterintuitive to delay seeking agreement, but it's counterproductive to start there. Mike and I have learned this (and periodically had to relearn this) the hard way!

The apostle Paul doesn't bring up agreement until the fourth step, and even then, he calls for a very different approach from what most of us might expect. The words in New Testament Greek together translated "seek agreement," "agree," or "be like-minded" have interesting meanings: *Autos* means "self" and carries the idea of a backward wind, something that blows back onto something.[1] *Phroneō* means "to exercise the mind," "to entertain or have a sentiment or opinion; by implication, to be (mentally) disposed (more or less earnestly in a certain direction); intensively, to interest oneself in (with concern or obedience): set the affection on."[2]

In short, the words might be understood to mean to "be of one mind," "mind yourself (or yourselves)," "intensely interest yourself in yourselves," or "set your affection on one another." The concept that it brings to my mind is intensely interesting yourself in another person's view, being concerned about the other person so much that the goodwill blows back toward you, drawing the other person toward you.

Unfortunately, when we think about seeking agreement, we tend to equate that with persuading another person to come around to our viewpoint, proving ourselves right. Instead, 2 Corinthians describes an intense interest in or affection for another person; seeking common ground; a movement of both people.

When Charles was "visiting" in our home, Mike and I focused on his needs. During the time we were comforting him, coming alongside him, the Holy Spirit was working too. Charles came to realize that his situation wouldn't allow him to move home without any input from me or Mike. He also realized that he wanted whatever time he had left to be spent with his family.

In short, we were coming to agreement with one another almost naturally. Charles and his beloved dachshund, Rex, settled in. The hot mess of a fight that had started the moment the doctors had begun discussing releasing Charles from the hospital melted away as we walked through the first three steps of fighting well. The more we carved out time and activities to create joy in the midst of a truly painful and heartbreaking journey of terminal illness, the more we aimed at restoring as much as possible what Charles and Mike most feared losing (Charles's independence and dignity, Mike's time and connection with his dad), the more we comforted one another by coming alongside each other, the closer to agreement we came just as a natural part of the process.

Paul drives this home elsewhere with the command to "do nothing from selfish ambition or conceit" but "in humility count others more significant than yourselves" (Philippians 2:3). If we really do that, there will be few fights that require going to the fourth step, let alone fights that can't be resolved in the fourth step. When we humbly aim for restoration and actively comfort each other, the agreement process is a natural outgrowth, almost a by-product, of the first three steps.

James confirms this when he writes, "What causes quarrels and what causes fights among you? Is it not this, that your passions are at war within you? You desire and do not have, so you murder. You covet and cannot obtain, so you fight and quarrel. You do not have, because you do not ask" (James 4:1-2).

If we're confident enough in God's love and our standing as His children, selfless enough because of His forgiveness, we can give way on almost anything for the sake of agreement—except what would dishonor God.

No one is perfect, so whenever two of us are trying to reach an agreement, we usually both need to move. Until we're changed "in the twinkling of an eye" to be like Jesus (see 1 Corinthians 15:52), none of us is fully in agreement with God—no matter how much more right we seem than the other person.

In fact, there are areas and issues on which agreeing to disagree is actually a good thing. If you can agree to disagree, you have reached agreement. However, if one of you feels angry, cheated, or resentful, you haven't really agreed.

Sinful Behavior

Agreeing with each other, however, can never come at the sacrifice of honoring God.

As a husband, you can agree to do more, expect less, eat crow, give up things you want, do things you hate, or change the most innocent-but-annoying-to-her habit. However, you can't condone sin. When a disagreement involves a sinful behavior, you must address it. That's why this step has some clearly defined substeps to help you when agreement is elusive.

Matthew 18:15-18 spells out the steps for seeking agreement in difficult situations:

> "If your brother sins against you, go and tell him his fault, between you and him alone. If he listens to you, you have gained your brother. But if he does not listen, take one or two others along with you, that every charge may be

> established by the evidence of two or three witnesses. If he refuses to listen to them, tell it to the church. And if he refuses to listen even to the church, let him be to you as a Gentile and a tax collector. Truly, I say to you, whatever you bind on earth shall be bound in heaven, and whatever you loose on earth shall be loosed in heaven."

If you've tried to reach agreement in private—just the two of you—but can't, you need help. When agreement can't be reached even after you've done all you know to do to model Christ's love, you must be willing to fight well by going through the steps Jesus Himself outlines in Matthew 18. You might also consider engaging the assistance of a Christian counselor.

Mark 11:25 commands us to forgive right in the middle of prayer: "Whenever you stand praying, forgive, if you have anything against anyone, so that your Father also who is in heaven may forgive you your trespasses." Matthew 5:23 insists that we even leave unfinished business at the altar of God to go be reconciled to a person who "has something against" us.

You can't just sweep it under the rug. Reconciliation is urgent business.

When we were not only out of agreement with Him but also in total rebellion, Jesus bore the cross for us. He knew the battle wasn't with flesh and blood, but the battle did require that He sacrifice *His* flesh and blood—for us. He didn't make it okay for us to stay in our sin; He made a way for us to be free of our sin, to be like Him. The kind of self-sacrifice modeled after His, made so that we can create agreement, is the work of a husband empowered by the Holy Spirit.

Countdown Journal

How is seeking agreement different from proving you're right or trying to make your fiancée change?

How will you proactively overcome areas of disagreement?

Anniversary Reflection

What issues have cropped up this year that still have you and your wife in disagreement?

What steps from Matthew 18:15-18 have you taken?

What do you need to do to reach agreement on these issues?

DAY 4

Live in Peace (Step 5 for Fighting Well)

When Mike and I had been married for about fourteen years, a friend who had been married for just a couple of years told me about a shocking revelation she had experienced in a Sunday school class. The class leader had made the statement that most men mistakenly and sincerely believe that a big argument (or a series of little arguments) between a husband and wife indicates that something is seriously wrong with the marriage.

She said that several women in the class, including her, were incredulous. So the leader asked any men who felt that way and were willing to admit it to raise their hands. To her surprise, her husband raised his hand and even expressed relief when most of the other men did the same. They all seemed surprised to find that arguments are, in fact, a normal part of a good, even great, marriage.

I told her that I, too, was puzzled by the men's misconception. I suggested that a few more years of marital experience would have alleviated that feeling for them but at least the class cleared up that misunderstanding. She suggested I ask my husband, and I said confidently that we had been married quite a bit longer and that he knew better than to think that happily married people—even those in great marriages—don't argue.

Later, I told Mike about the conversation, and as my story unfolded, his eyes widened, and he cut me off to say, "Man, that makes me feel better!"

Your marriage *will* have drama, trauma, and trouble. Your wife *will* make mistakes and sin, and so will you. You'll disagree and argue with each other. You're still a beloved son of God married to a beloved daughter of God. The fact that you argue and fuss doesn't mean something is fundamentally wrong with your marriage. It means you're human beings trying to live authentic lives together. When iron sharpens iron, sparks fly.

We tend to wrongly believe that living in peace should be the natural and normal first state. We falsely think that restoring and comforting should only be necessary if something goes terribly wrong and breaks the natural order of living in peace. Before the fall, that might have been true. But since the day sin entered the world, broken is the natural and usual state of relationships. Indeed, every relationship recorded in any detail in Scripture and history—except the relationship among Jesus, God the Father, and the Holy Spirit—is broken.

Peace Is Active

Step 5 in fighting well is to *seek peace*. It comes after the work of rejoicing, restoring, comforting, and creating agreement. Real peace is possible only because of Jesus' willingness to fight well for us against the true enemy: "I have said these things to you, that in me you may have peace. In the world you will have tribulation. But take heart; I have overcome the world" (John 16:33).

Note that God's peace is not passive. It's an active force in our lives. According to Philippians 4:7, "the peace of God, which surpasses all understanding, will guard your hearts and your minds in Christ Jesus."

As the husband, you're called to be willing to lay down your life, to give up your rights and freedoms for the good of your marriage and the glory of God, to sacrifice your preferences to keep peace, to overcome all the cultural pressure to exert your own will and way, and to honor Christ by honoring your wife. But if you focus on peace before the first four steps are complete, you're a peacekeeper, not a peacemaker.

If you seek peace without first rejoicing together, aiming for restoration, providing comfort, and seeking agreement, you're just avoiding. Peace is not the product of passivity.

There's a vast difference between the two. Peacekeeping is usually not even about true peace. *Peace* in Scripture refers to harmony, completeness, soundness, and contentment. Peacekeeping is more accurately identified as conflict avoidance. Peacekeeping lets issues fester, leaves conflicts unresolved. The harder you work at peacekeeping, the less you feel harmony, completeness, soundness, or contentment.

Real peace is active. Your God created you. He pursues you. He calls you. He leads you. He hems you in, going behind and before you (Psalm 139:5). He whispers to you. There's nothing passive about Him, and yet He is "the God of love and peace" (2 Corinthians 13:11).

Peacemaking requires completing the work of reconciliation. We can't have harmony with unresolved conflict. We can't enjoy contentment without restoration. We can't have soundness when sin is left unaddressed.

Jesus and Peter

In one of the most poignant peacemaking events in the Bible, Jesus seeks peace for and with Peter on the shore of the Sea of Galilee. Jesus, the One who has been wronged, the One who has just died and risen from the grave to save us all, initiates full reconciliation with Peter.

Remember the scene in John 21. Jesus, risen from the dead, has fixed breakfast for Peter and the disciples with him. He has called them in from fishing after helping them fill their nets. They've eaten together.

Then Jesus initiates reconciliation with Peter, the one who denied Him three times before the rooster crowed (see Matthew 26:69-75). He doesn't wait for Peter to apologize or even ask for an apology. He instead gives Peter the chance to affirm his love for Him—three times. And each time, Jesus gives Peter encouragement to put his love into action.

"Simon, son of John, do you love me more than these?"

"Yes, Lord; you know that I love you."

"Feed my lambs."

"Simon, son of John, do you love me?"

"Yes, Lord; you know that I love you."

"Tend my sheep."

"Simon, son of John, do you love me?"

"Lord, you know everything; you know that I love you."

"Feed my sheep" (John 21:15-17).

Can you imagine the release, the peace that flooded Peter? I can. Mike can.

"Mike, do you love me?" I often ask.

"Yes, Leann; I love you."

He has said it hundreds of times, and each time it strengthens our reconciliation.

But the enemy never quits. Even in this moment, after Jesus has overcome the grave, and after Peter has declared his love for Jesus three times, the enemy throws down another challenge. He still wants Peter, and if he can't keep him tangled up in the guilt of betrayal, he will try to trip him up with comparison.

In the very next moments, after having just experienced the restorative grace of Jesus, Peter turns his focus to someone else:

> Peter turned and saw the disciple whom Jesus loved following them, the one who also had leaned back against him during the supper and had said, "Lord, who is it that

> is going to betray you?" When Peter saw him, he said to Jesus, "Lord, what about this man?" Jesus said to him, "If it is my will that he remain until I come, what is that to you? You follow me!"
>
> JOHN 21:20-22

We do that, don't we? We hear Jesus speaking to us, calling us to live for Him, and we point at someone else and ask, "What about her?"

The Word tells us how to express our love for God, how to put that love into action. It instructs, "Husbands should love their wives as their own bodies. He who loves his wife loves himself. For no one ever hated his own flesh, but nourishes and cherishes it, just as Christ does the church" (Ephesians 5:28-29).

Yet before we face even the first challenge to that effort, almost before we hear the end of the sentence, we say, *Lord, what about her? What about my wife? Shouldn't she be doing ________________?*

Jesus speaks to Peter, and His words speak to us, in that moment: "What is that to you? You follow me!" (John 21:22).

Our Story

I can often see myself in Peter's missteps. The impetuosity, the mercurial behavior, the rush to mistaken actions, the confidence that I would *never* . . . only to *never* like I never *nevered* before—just in time to hear the rooster crow.

Mike's and my walk with Jesus took us away from that dream house on the bayou and moved us to Alexandria, Louisiana. We didn't want to move. However, since then, we've had a great life in Alexandria. We've both had the opportunity to work with great employers and people. Our kids did well in school. Both our sons met their precious wives in Alexandria.

But Mike and I both love being near water, and we've dreamed of owning waterfront property. Once the kids were married, Mike and

I started wondering about the possibility of downsizing and finding a home on water.

This time, we didn't want to repeat the missteps we'd made before. We openly talked about what we wanted without shutting down when our views didn't fully align. We committed ourselves to praying together about our dream, regularly and especially before taking any action. I made a commitment that I wouldn't push Mike, that I would give input and be open about my feelings but that I would follow his lead. Mike made a commitment to lead, to be fully engaged even when it was uncomfortable.

We sold our house and moved into an apartment, believing it would be for a year, maybe eighteen months, while we looked for waterfront property.

We had barely moved into the apartment when we found a house I loved on Cane River for sale by owner. It ticked all the boxes, but Mike didn't think it was the right place because the drive was more than fifty minutes to his job and my business. I wasn't pushing; I was being gentle; I was trying to follow. We looked at that house several times. It quickly sold, but then the contract fell through and it came back on the market. I just knew it was because it was meant for us.

We looked at it again. I fell a bit more in love. Mike agreed that it was hitting all the checkboxes except for the drive, a drive that triggered memories of another time when he'd had to make a long commute that had wedged time between him and me, between him and home. I reminded myself to share my thoughts but not to push, to be gentle. I also reminded myself that God was not just speaking to me. What a struggle!

The Cane River house sold, and my resolve to be gentle wavered. A year turned into two. COVID-19 hit, and the housing market went crazy—waterfront property nearly doubled in price and was selling as fast as it hit the market. All our progress seemed to implode as we suddenly started comparing where we were (in an apartment with increasing rent and rapidly rising interest rates) to where we had been (in a big house with a yard and a pool, paying less than 3 percent interest).

Another year passed in that apartment, and I was doing all I could not to push, to be gentle and patient. My resolve started to seem unreasonable. *But, Lord,* I prayed, *what about him, what about Mike?* I went on. *Lord, Mike is really trying to lead, not to seek his own comfort in this, not to be passive. But, Lord, what about him?*

Jesus spoke to Peter, and His words spoke to me: *What is that to you? You follow Me!* I reminded myself, *Jesus knows the desire of my heart. He hears my prayer. Mike has heard me too. The Holy Spirit lives in both of us, and we've both committed to this path.* So I focused on praying often, being honest about my feelings as gently as I could, and praying more when I couldn't be gentle.

Here's what I've learned: Don't get distracted by what your wife should and shouldn't do. Her actions neither dictate nor justify yours. Neither your wife nor you have the final say. Even your own mistakes and sins and her mistakes and sins are subject to the truth that "for those who love God all things work together for good, for those who are called according to his purpose" (Romans 8:28). Hold on to that promise.

As a husband, you're making a covenant with God to hold fast to your wife and to love her as Christ loves the church. You're entering into an agreement that you will do good regardless of what happens, even when things are bad. No matter what your wife does or is called to do, Jesus says, *What is that to you? You follow Me!*

When we keep our focus on Jesus and measure ourselves only against Him and His will for our lives, we can truly seek peace with and for each other.

Countdown Journal

How is living in peace both part of "fighting a good fight" and the result of fighting well?

How does failing to fight well or even avoiding fights have a negative impact on living in peace?

Anniversary Reflection

What have you tended to sweep under the rug to maintain peace?

What are the dangers of that, and how can you overcome it?

DAY 3

Commit to Daily Affection

Mike and I have different love languages. There are only five of them, according to author Dr. Gary Chapman in his book *The Five Love Languages*. Mike's primary love language is gifts. His secondary is quality time. My primary love language is physical touch. My secondary is words of affirmation. You don't have to know much about the love languages or the book to guess how that plays out.

If I tell Mike all kinds of affirming things and hold his hand, he may very well enjoy it. But if I never buy him gifts or spend what he considers to be quality time with him, he won't feel loved. Likewise, if he showers me with gifts and tries to get me to watch college football with him every Saturday but rarely touches me or tells me how he feels about me or compliments me, I don't feel loved. In fact, when that happens, I feel used or taken for granted.

Your love language also affects the way you address apologies. In the past, Mike would buy flowers or small gifts when he needed to apologize, and it irritated me. It felt as if he was trying to take the easy way out by glossing over the hurt with a gift. Then every time I looked at the gift or flowers I was reminded of the hurt that he wouldn't make the effort to address. On the other hand, my apologies come with hugs and words—lots of words—just as I would like to receive. Mike would much rather get a new bag of coffee and an invitation to brew a cup for us both to enjoy on the back porch.

We've learned a bit about speaking the language the other needs to hear. I have a box full of letters and cards from Mike. Every Christmas for years now I've found a handwritten, multipage letter, usually on lined yellow Uline notepad paper, in my stocking. He recaps our year and reminisces and says something sweet about me and our relationship. I treasure those letters, and the words he writes affirming our love are the ones I read, and need to read, over and over. Those words fill my heart. They soothe me.

I've gotten better at giving gifts. Mike has a bunch of wristwatches, many bought by me, some bought by our sons. He loves them. One more is never too many.

Gifting well has challenged me in several ways. The hardest part has been overcoming my tendency to bargain shop. While it still feels a bit too easy to go to a men's store and pick out a nice shirt or two, I make the extra effort to go to his favorite men's shop and pay full price for the brand he loves in the latest style. Though the siren call of the clearance rack beckons powerfully, I stand strong, because his love language matters, and I refuse to buy his gifts the way I shop for myself.

I'm also better now about joining him for quality time. He even gives me credit when he watches football, commenting on the game to me, though I'm reading something and not really watching. He enjoys hanging out on the back porch together, reading or praying or just looking at the water. (Yes, we finally got the house fronting the river.) He enjoys riding bikes together. He usually leads, and we don't really chat.

The Need for Affection

Immediately after listing the steps for resolving conflict in 2 Corinthians 13, Paul adds this imperative: "Greet one another with a holy kiss" (2 Corinthians 13:12). This isn't so much a step of fighting well or reconciling as it is the celebration of being reconciled.

This is not the kiss of Song of Solomon 1:2: "Let him kiss me with the kisses of his mouth! For your love is better than wine." That form of kissing will continue to play a key part in your relationship—but we're saving that discussion for tomorrow. The kiss in 2 Corinthians 13 is the kiss with which Christians were accustomed to welcoming or dismissing their companions in the faith as a sign of fraternal affection.

In several verses in the New Testament, we're encouraged to show genuine, comfortable, mutual affection. Even the word translated "greet" here, which can mean "to welcome" or even "to embrace" communicates affection. The picture here is of a warm, affectionate, inviting welcome.[1]

Writing that phrase reminds me of my grandparents, Big Momma and Big Daddy—Granville and Louella Martin. I can't remember a single time I was ever with them that didn't begin and end with a hug and kiss—a big bear hug and an intentional kiss. If I didn't run directly to Big Momma when we met, she would call out, "Where's my hug and kiss?" I loved the way Big Momma and Big Daddy made me feel. Those hugs and kisses gave me a sense of being genuinely liked as well as loved.

Take time every day, several times a day, to give your wife a hug and a kiss. Some days that will be what she most needs from you—just a reminder of your *agape* love for her. In this you will be modeling Christ's love for the church—deep, unchanging love.

Several times every day, wrap your arms around your wife, rest her head on your chest, and remind her that you genuinely like her, that your affection for her is powerful and based on more than sexual attraction.

As so often happens, science has just begun to realize some of the physiological benefits of something commended in Scripture. In 2009, Arizona State University communications professor Kory

Floyd and some colleagues studied the physiological impact of kissing and other expressions of affection. The study revealed that kissing can "improve your health, benefit your well-being, and improve your intimate relationships."[2] An article reporting on the study in *Psychology Today* states,

> At the end of the study, the kissing group [as distinguished from the control group that did not intentionally increase kissing] in fact stated they felt less stressed and more satisfied in their relationship. Importantly, for their health, their cholesterol levels (the "bad" kind) decreased as well. Compared to the control group, the couples in the kissing group also reported that they exercised more, argued less, had less conflict, and understood each other better.[3]

In an article published on the *U.S. News & World Report* website in 2016, Stacey Colino writes about the benefits of hugs.[4] She references a 2015 study involving 404 healthy adults during which Carnegie Mellon University researched the effects of hugs on our susceptibility to catching the common cold after exposure to a virus. The study showed an increase in resistance to the illness for participants who received more hugs and noted that 32 percent of the impact was due to the "stress-buffering effects of hugging."

According to psychologist Tiffany Field, director of the Touch Research Institute at the University of Miami School of Medicine, who is quoted in the article, "When you're hugging or cuddling with someone, [he or she is] stimulating pressure receptors under your skin in a way that leads to a cascade of events including an increase in vagal activity, which puts you in a relaxed state." Colino notes a theory that the stimulation of the vagus nerve by this "cascade of events . . . triggers an increase in oxytocin levels."

Oxytocin, she explains, is a hormone that influences mood and behavior, even playing a bonding role in relationships, as evidenced specifically between a mother and her child; the hormone is released after birth and promotes feelings of attachment. Interestingly, Field notes that the quality of the hug matters: "If you get a flimsy hug, that's not going to do it. . . . You need a firm hug."

Affection changes us on a physical and emotional level. We need to receive physical evidence of affection. We need to give physical evidence of affection. Studies and anecdotal evidence show that we need to give and receive twenty-to-sixty-second hugs intentionally and regularly. Stress is relieved, powerful endorphins release, moods improve, and relationships are strengthened.

But affection is also expressed in words, in time, in gifts, and in actions. For some like Mike, some of those other ways are more important than physical touch. You probably already know how your fiancée is most comfortable expressing affection. I hope she knows your primary love language too. Don't assume either though. Take time to ask her what makes her feel loved, what expressions of affection mean the most to her. Be intentional in telling her how she can speak most clearly to *your* heart.

If you haven't already read the book *The Five Love Languages*, spend the next five minutes taking the quiz[5] to learn your primary love language. Encourage your fiancée to do the same. Then set a goal of reading the book together in the next year. Grab hold of ways to speak each other's love languages and commit to doing them often.

A Test of Love

Several years ago, Mike and I became pretty consistent bike riders, and I learned to really enjoy it. We would cruise around town, Mike leading and me listening to an audiobook, logging thirty-plus miles a week.

One spring, Mike started to notice that longer rides were creating some pain. It got bad enough that he cut back on our rides together. After several months, he went to see a doctor.

One of the tests the doctor ran required anesthesia, and afterward, Mike began to wake up in the recovery room, loopy and funny. He made some goofy comments that made me snort just as the curtain slid back. We were still giggling when the doctor said, "We found a large mass—not exactly what we were expecting."

Mike immediately sobered up and looked straight at me. I held his gaze as the doctor continued talking in sentences neither of us could really hear—something about CT scans and biopsies, likely malignancy, possible metastasis.

"God's got this," I said.

Without blinking, Mike said, "I know."

"Stupid fig tree," I added.

He smiled even as tears welled up in his eyes. We knew in that moment that we were facing a horrible disease, but we also knew that Jesus promised that we can curse a tree so that it withers, never to bear fruit again. We can command mountains to be moved.

When the nurses gave him the prep he had to drink for the battery of tests about to start, they finally all stepped out, and we were alone for the first time since the doctor had spoken. I leaned over the bed rail. He wrapped his arms around me and kissed me. Both our hearts settled a bit.

Marriage needs to be filled with affection, and you'll need to be intentional about not letting familiarity rob you of the joy of expressing affection every day, several times a day. Start your morning with affection. Every time you separate for work, slow down long enough for a sixty-second hug and a goodbye kiss. When you come home, no matter how your day has gone, go to her and take her into your arms. Relish the fact that you're married to the one your soul loves. Remind her how her love makes you happy. Science and Scripture both point out the importance of affection, so hug and kiss her often. As seventeenth-century poet Robert Herrick wrote:

Give me a kiss, and to that kiss a score ;
Then to that twenty add a hundred more :
A thousand to that hundred : so kiss on,
To make that thousand up a million.

> *Treble that million, and when that is done*
> *Let's kiss afresh, as when we first begun.*[6]

Or as the great twenty-first-century philosopher Si Robertson said in an interview:

> What I tell young couples that are getting married is: you're going to have quarrels, and on some things, you're just going to have to agree to disagree. And when you go to bed at night, kiss each other and tell each other that you love each other. Don't go to bed mad. Life is too short. Keep it simple.[7]

Countdown Journal

Even when you're tired, angry, frustrated, or distracted, what commitment will you make when it comes to kissing your soon-to-be wife, confirming your affection for her in a physical and tender way?

How are your needs for affection and hers different? What's her love language?

Anniversary Reflection

What do you need to forgive in yourself and your wife to keep bitterness from slowing down your affection?

What expressions of love mean the most to your wife?

DAY 2

Celebrate Sex

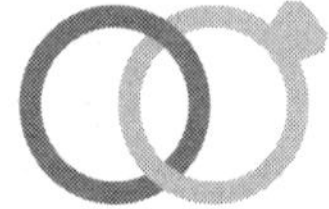

Mike and I didn't read a single book about sex until after we were married. My personal physician wasn't helpful; he assumed everyone from the age of puberty and up was, no doubt, actively having sex and that putting every menstruating girl on oral birth control was his sole responsibility. Our ministers growing up didn't broach the subject of sex except to condemn it outside marriage, and our parents' input ranged from not talking about it to being negative.

I hope your education has been better and that this chapter will help.

If you started reading this collection of reminders twenty-one days before your wedding, then today you're getting ready for the rehearsal and wrapping up the final details for the ceremony. Tomorrow will be the last time you kiss her as your fiancée. The next time you kiss her, she'll be your wife. Tomorrow will be the last time you sleep in separate homes, the last night before you celebrate the joy of God-designed, God-ordained, God-blessed sex. You read that right. God-blessed sex! Awesome, intimate, precious, binding, comforting, stress-relieving, exciting, thrilling sex!

Lies and myths about sex abound. Our enemy, the father of lies, wants you to believe them all. The nonbelieving world and, sadly, even many believers think that marriage is optional but sex is unavoidable, an expected activity, often without marriage on the radar—that sex is just a part of dating, a personal choice with no boundaries.

Like every good thing, sex can be abused or misused. It can be treated as shameful, or it can become the idol served. At any of those extremes, it does powerful damage.

Mike and I made a point of changing the narrative around sex as we raised our sons. In our families of origin, Mike rarely saw his mom and dad express affection, and they never spoke of sex. In my family, sex was listed as pretty much the greatest sin, only made okay when it became required in marriage. Mike and I talked openly in our family about sex, both the biblical plan for sex in marriage versus the secular view and the joy of love expressed sexually as God intended versus the heartbreak of sex used as a weapon or tool. We were openly affectionate in front of our kids but tried not to make it cringey.

Your family may have been open about sex as well, but in many families, sex is either a taboo subject or a source of raunchy jokes. Often either the conversations are open but bawdy, not honoring sex as a gift from God, or the topic is taboo and makes sex seem like a bad thing.

What the Bible Says

The Bible has a lot to say about sex, both holy sex and sex that's destructive. Almost every book in the Old Testament includes teaching or guidance on sex. A father's admonitions about sex and advice for his son fill Proverbs. Hosea is a story wrapped around sex at all the extremes—prostitution, sex within the sanctity of marriage, the betrayal and damage of sex outside marriage, and the dangers of sex used for control and destruction. The Song of Solomon vividly and poetically describes the intimacy of marital sex and compares it to the intimacy of God's love for us.

You can find lots of great biblically based resources about marital intimacy online and in books. Let me recommend two books that would be great next reads for you and your wife by therapist Clifford Penner and his wife, Joyce, a registered nurse: *The Married Guy's Guide to Great Sex* and *Enjoy! The Gift of Sexual Pleasure for Women*. The Focus on the Family website includes lots of good articles by the Penners and others. Jimmy Evans and his wife have a guide for a vision retreat for married couples, and they strongly recommend taking retreats focused on your vision for sex in your marriage.[1]

Mike and I have certainly seen the powerfully destructive impact of sex outside God's plan. Infidelity can destroy a marriage. Even when a couple commits to reconciliation, the damage of infidelity wreaks havoc that must be addressed.

Pornography is another destructive attack on marriages. Yet another common and painful struggle involves differences in sexual desire or preferences. All these attacks come insidiously and often take root even in marriages where both the husband and the wife are committed Jesus followers. Until you know that to be true, you won't build the protection and alarms into your relationship that you need.

The core truth for you to embrace is that God Himself designed sex as a precious, fun, intimate connection shared only, shamelessly and joyfully, with your wife.

In the perfection of paradise, before sin entered the world, God blessed the first couple and told them to have sex. God Himself instituted marriage, and He created sexual intimacy to be the joyful connection between husband and wife. They were fully exposed to each other without any shame.

One verse that goes right to the core of celebrating sex is Hebrews 13:4: "Let marriage be held in honor among all, and let the marriage bed be undefiled, for God will judge the sexually immoral and adulterous." While sex outside marriage bears judgment, Scripture commands that marriage is to be honored and clearly states that the *bed*, or sexual intercourse *in marriage*, is *undefiled*, which means unsoiled, pure, and free from sin.

Your relationship as a husband and wife includes intimacy of every kind—from knowing each other's emotional tendencies to favorite foods to romantic gestures to favorite sex positions. Scripture shows that sex in marriage is integral to the health of your relationship and helping each other stay faithful. First Corinthians 7:3-5 teaches the fundamental principle of mutual support between a husband and wife for each other's sexual and physical needs and the importance of being responsive to each other sexually:

> The husband should give to his wife her conjugal rights, and likewise the wife to her husband. For the wife does not have authority over her own body, but the husband does. Likewise the husband does not have authority over his own body, but the wife does.
>
> 1 CORINTHIANS 7:3-4

This passage is a powerful contradiction to those who falsely believe that Christian marriage allows for any level of inequality. The husband doesn't have authority over his own body; the wife does. The wife doesn't have authority over her own body; the husband does. Submit to each other. Love your wife as your own body. All these truths about God's guidance for marriage point to a place of mutual safety, love, compassion, and joy.

Paul continues in this same passage to point out that the only reason husbands and wives should abstain from sex is to spend more time in prayer, and he's clear that those times must be limited, agreed to by you both: "Do not deprive one another, except perhaps by agreement for a limited time, that you may devote yourselves to prayer; but then come together again, so that Satan may not tempt you because of your lack of self-control" (1 Corinthians 7:5).

Scripture is also clear that monogamous sex is fun, sensual, and full of joy:

> Drink water from your own cistern,
>   flowing water from your own well.

Should your springs be scattered abroad,
  streams of water in the streets?
Let them be for yourself alone,
  and not for strangers with you.
Let your fountain be blessed,
  and rejoice in the wife of your youth,
  a lovely deer, a graceful doe.
Let her breasts fill you at all times with delight;
  be intoxicated always in her love.

PROVERBS 5:15-19

You have captivated my heart, my sister, my bride;
  you have captivated my heart with one glance of your eyes,
  with one jewel of your necklace.
How beautiful is your love, my sister, my bride!
  How much better is your love than wine,
  and the fragrance of your oils than any spice!

SONG OF SOLOMON 4:9-10

It goes down smoothly for my beloved,
  gliding over lips and teeth.

I am my beloved's,
  and his desire is for me.

Come, my beloved,
  let us go out into the fields
  and lodge in the villages;
let us go out early to the vineyards
  and see whether the vines have budded,
whether the grape blossoms have opened
  and the pomegranates are in bloom.
There I will give you my love.

> The mandrakes give forth fragrance,
>   and beside our doors are all choice fruits,
> new as well as old,
>   which I have laid up for you, O my beloved.
>
> SONG OF SOLOMON 7:9-13

Scripture teaches at least five core principles about sex in the context of marriage:

1. God created it as a blessing to be shared exclusively between one man and the one woman to whom he is married.
2. Marriage is honorable, and sex in marriage is undefiled and pure.
3. Husbands and wives are to be mutually supportive of and responsive to each other sexually.
4. The only time a husband and wife should refrain from sex is for limited periods, decided together, so each person can devote more time to prayer.
5. Married sex is intended to be joyful—to be so much fun!

Within those clear and simple boundaries comes freedom to grow in intimacy and to enjoy sex for a lifetime. My hope is that you've had a person in your life who has taught a positive attitude about God-blessed sex and has been open with you. I also hope you'll commit to reading at least one of those books I mentioned this year with your new wife. Then relax and take time to be romantic. Focus on pleasing each other (not necessarily always at the same time).

That first core truth testifies to God's intention for marriage. The second is also found right there in the beginning: The enemy wants to kill, steal, and destroy relationships (see Genesis 3; John 10:10). Satan's very first move against humanity was to divide and separate. He didn't approach Adam and Eve together. He attacked one, and through that attack he trapped both. The almost immediate result of that first sin, shame, became a wedge between them and between them and God.

Sad Facts

We live in a natural world under both natural and supernatural attack. God designed your marriage as a place of honesty, companionship, help, joy, sex, and unity. Left to the natural course without intentional care and repair, everything declines, including—maybe especially—relationships. Supernaturally, we have a relentless enemy who works hard to destroy everything good and holy. The enemy hates everything about marriage. God is for you, and the enemy opposes you. Don't miss this truth: Your marriage is under attack, and sex can easily become a powerful weapon.

Here are some of the indicators of the brokenness of many marriages:

- According to a study published in *The New England Journal of Medicine*, approximately 40 to 50 percent of married couples report having experienced some form of sexual dysfunction or dissatisfaction at some point in their relationship.[2]
- One survey indicates that about one in three couples reports sexual problems such as lack of desire, communication issues, or physical difficulties.[3]
- Studies show that about 80 percent of couples report experiencing a sexual desire discrepancy, where one partner has a higher or lower level of sexual desire than the other, leading to potential frustration and tension in the relationship.[4]
- A longitudinal study suggests that about 70 percent of couples report a decline in sexual activity after having children, mainly due to factors such as exhaustion, changes in intimacy, and shifts in priorities.[5]
- Approximately 23 percent of men and 19 percent of women report having engaged in extramarital sex during their marriage.[6]
- About 43 percent of women and 31 percent of men experience some form of sexual dysfunction in their marriages. Common

issues include erectile dysfunction, premature ejaculation, low libido, and pain during intercourse.[7]

- Psychological factors are strongly linked to sexual dissatisfaction. According to the International Society for Sexual Medicine, "research has consistently shown associations between sexual dysfunction and mental health conditions such as depression and anxiety."[8]

Those statistics, as concerning as they are, probably understate the problem. Many couples never report their struggles. They simply struggle alone, which is, in itself, probably another damaging ploy of the enemy. No one goes into marriage okay with becoming one of those statistics, nor should they. But you need to know these realities so you know the risks and how to prevent the problem. Let these be a sort of risk advisory, a clarion call to take steps now to be on the other side of those statistics. Be a champion for marriage. Fight for your wife and for your marriage. Take steps to be sure you're part of the positive percentages.

What to Do

What can you do to maintain a healthy sexual relationship in your marriage? Consider the following:

- Ferret out any sexual lies or myths that either of you struggle with so you both enjoy functional and satisfying sex together.
- Work on your communication styles, improving weaknesses and reinforcing strengths, so you can easily and often talk about your sex life and especially so you can together refute the lies and misunderstandings that the enemy will continually feed and promote to you.
- Commit to working on your physical health—individually and as a couple.

- If there's a desire discrepancy, address it as you would if one of you lacked a desire to eat often enough to be healthy. Don't allow it to become insulting or be taken as a personal failure of either person.

In the first years of our marriage, Mike and I had sex often, and both of us initiated it. He had no doubt I found him attractive. He left no doubt in my mind that he found me sexy.

Like many couples, we experienced a traumatic shift when we went from being a couple to having a family. It felt as if sex came to a screeching halt when I reached about six months pregnant. In hindsight, it's easier to see how worries for his wife and unborn baby, as scientifically unfounded as they are, can affect a young husband. In the moment, when the husband is hesitant, the enemy will convince a young wife that extra weight has made her too frumpy or that she's lost some of her allure or that she looks as tired as she feels. When the wife hesitates or withdraws, a young husband may feel like he's losing her love, like he's no longer a priority.

Since I had a C-section, we had to delay sex eight weeks longer than planned. I continued to tell myself that Mike's sudden reserve was about protecting me, fear of hurting me physically, but I worried more and more that it was something deeper, and I let that hurt grow.

Looking back now, the smartest choice we made was to take a vacation as a couple. With guilt, we planned a trip to Mexico and asked Mike's parents to keep Patrick for a few days when he was a toddler. We both remember that vacation vividly: worrying about being away from the baby, feeling selfish for wanting a break, crying all the way to the airport, *and* indulging in three gloriously uninterrupted nights of sleep that extended well past sunrise. Dancing in the rain. Eating slow and relaxing meals. Having sex without worrying about waking the baby. Having sex without having to debate whether we should just get some desperately needed sleep instead. We should have done that kind of trip more often.

We've faced medical issues that have hurt our sex life. I mentioned that C-sections mean extra weeks of restrictions. Thyroid issues affect libido. Cancer treatment definitely disrupts normal patterns of intimacy. Don't give way to the attack of the enemy that will come during those times. Consult with doctors, and take their advice. Go to counseling—and go back again as needed. Don't hesitate to seek out whatever help you need for your physical, mental, and sexual health. Fight for each other.

Don't let the enemy get a foothold. If you're the one with less desire, remind yourself that you're the one your wife loves, the one she wants, and she cannot relieve the appetite her love for you creates with any other person. With every effort, fight this demonic attack. Fan the flame of your desires for her by focusing on all her best characteristics. Help her learn how to encourage your desire. Don't leave her alone and rejected. Reassure her of your love, your attraction to her. Find out her preferred frequency, and don't be hesitant to set aside time on your calendar. Then keep those appointments.

If you're the one with greater desire, remind yourself that differences are normal, and for 80 percent of couples, this difference causes enough pain that they share it with counselors or doctors (or survey takers). Talk to your wife about your needs. Don't fall into the enemy's trap of *If my wife really loved me, she would* ______________. Remember, we all have our own love languages, and we all have different preferences. Instead, ask how you can fan the flames for your wife, and help her discover how to speak your love language(s). Fight for your sexual health.

You have a lifetime to practice—and what fun the practicing can be! So, once you're married, bring on the romance.

Soften the lights.

Let go of any preconceptions.

Turn all your sexual fantasies and thoughts toward your wife.

Put on a little sensual music.

Take your time, and pop the cork on some chilled champagne. (After all, Jesus made sure there was plenty of wine at the wedding in Cana!)

Countdown Journal

What are the five most important aspects of sex for you? Discuss them with your fiancée.

1.

2.

3.

4.

5.

What are the five most important aspects of sex for her—according to her?

1.

2.

3.

4.

5.

Anniversary Reflection

How are you keeping sex a pleasurable priority for both of you?

Are there any boundaries you need to shore up to protect your commitment to each other?

DAY 1

Begin and End Everything with Jesus

As mentioned earlier, we did finally leave behind that cramped apartment, and I realized that God had placed us there for the exact season we needed small. He has always given us what we've needed when we've needed it. We've only begun to understand that. This growing realization settles my heart more every day.

I posted something like this on Facebook the day I could clearly see why God had kept us in the apartment for that season of small:

> One month in our new home; today is the first day I have sat on our back porch long enough to enjoy the serenity here. The leaves seem to fall constantly, only a few at a time, but every second one or two are flip-floating to the ground—until just now. Just now, the air has gone completely still. The only sound is the crackle of the fireplace. Somewhere behind me the sun is setting on the other side of the house, but the overcast skies make it feel less like dimming sunlight and more like a deepening of gray, falling almost purple as twilight nears. The water of the

oxbow ripples just enough to remind me that around the corner the Red River flows south.

He sits with me here this fading afternoon; in the quiet, I feel Him near me. He has run with me in the chaos; He has fought for me in the struggles; He has strengthened me when I've faltered. I know He is present, omnipresent. Yet, here in the quiet, I can take a moment to know He is here, to focus on His presence. "Be still, and know that I am God" (Psalm 46:10). Why is it so hard to do that? Why do we do it so seldom?

This is the season of big. I can feel it coming, see evidence of it around me in this house, but we so needed small for the last three years, even though we didn't know it. He did. When we prayed that He would lead us, that either the house would sell or we would settle into living there until retirement, He brought two offers in under two days.

When we prayed that He would help us find a decent place to rent (just for a year or less, we firmly believed), He moved us just a couple of doors down from Colten and Lydia and gave us the sweetest year with them as neighbors before they moved to Nashville. There He gave us more time. No yard to mow. No pool to clean. Way fewer bedrooms and bathrooms to clean. We had fewer rooms to be separate, working on our own. We had too little space to have people over or host showers and parties.

In the too little, in the season of small, we discovered the power of reading the Bible aloud together every day. We discovered the impact of praying together every morning—longer than just a blessing over a meal—sharing with one another and with God our concerns and dreams and praise. We didn't know what was coming; we didn't realize what He was preparing us to face. We just thought we were waiting to find a house.

When the diagnosis came back—malignant, aggressive cancer—we did *not* think, *God has been preparing us for this.* We did *not* think, *This is why.* We couldn't think of much at all. But in the moment that the first doctor said, "We found a mass," our eyes met and I said, "God's got us."

After the first few days of chemo, when the poison we use as medicine shredded the artery into Mike's heart, I didn't think, *Thank God we don't have to worry about mowing.* In fact, I don't remember thinking about the apartment at all, the house we were hunting for, work, or any of the things on which we focus most of our time.

We focused on what really matters—the people we love—one another, our family, and the God who would heal him or take him home. Our Father had thought of the other things: not having to worry about the lawn or the house or the mortgage that had exceeded our rent—all the things that made the year of treatment and surgery and recovery easier.

Our season of small wasn't just about the apartment. During that time, two of the biggest small things I can imagine came into our world—a first grandson and another pregnancy that became a second grandson. What bright spots those two small babies became during an overcast year, bookending Mike's diagnosis and his healing.

I have spent the afternoon pondering that season of small and knowing that the One who sits with me in this quiet gave us that season because He knew what we needed; He knows what we need.

As I write this, the darkness has become as pervasive as the quiet was earlier—the fire now the only light. The quiet has given way to movement. The breeze has picked up; leaves rustle and twigs snap. The neighbor's dogs bark and howl, likely at a possum; Mike has returned. I hear him clanking dishes in the kitchen.

> Even though the quiet has left, He is still here with me; He is always near. In the darkness, He is near. In the quiet, He is near. In the small, He is near. In the waiting room when a doctor tells you your husband likely won't make it, He is near. A year later, sitting on the back porch of a house that was only a dream, He is near. In every moment, He is near. In every season, this moment is His moment.[1]

Keeping Jesus First

That has been our recent journey through the seasons of married life. But today is the last day of *your* twenty-one-day countdown to the start of your marriage. In just one day, you marry her, the one person you love more than any other. What a blessing you're about to receive! What an incredible journey you're about to begin!

Because you and I believe Jesus is the Alpha and the Omega, the beginning and the end, my encouragement to you began with a focus on Jesus and ends with a focus on Jesus.

Never forget that God does not accept second place in our hearts. In the first written command, inscribed in stone, God asserted, "You shall have no other gods before me" (Exodus 20:3). According to Jesus, the greatest command is "Hear, O Israel: The Lord our God, the Lord is one. And you shall love the Lord your God with all your heart and with all your soul and with all your mind and with all your strength" (Mark 12:29-30).

In the marriage of Adam and Eve and every marriage since, trouble that damages our relationships finds its root in letting something, anything, come before God. The very first sin resulted because Adam and Eve listened to the serpent instead of God. Abraham and Sarah let doubt take their trust away from God; having a child became more important than honoring God. Abraham hid behind his wife's beauty because he feared Pharaoh instead of trusting God for protection. Gomer, the personification of Israel, sold herself into prostitution—choosing lovers who abandoned and abused her over the bridegroom who protected and redeemed her. Michal valued public image above ardent worship of God. David committed adultery and eventually murder to fill the void when he wasn't serving God. Solomon, the wisest man to ever live, the man God counted worthy of building His Temple, allowed the inanimate gods of his many wives to distract his heart from the one true God.

The current worldview takes this to a whole new level—not only allowing everything to come between us and God but also ousting God altogether, replacing Him with self-love, greed, and immediate gratification of every kind. Even many Christians have ceased to take seriously His commands, promises, and warnings.

In marriage, you can come to believe you're honoring God even though your wife has become your savior. If you bend God's will to your wife's or manipulate your wife to your will rather than God's, neither of those actions honors Him. One makes your wife the master; the other asserts your self as the master.

> **Satan baits us to swing to one of two destructive extremes—making the other person our focus or our own will the focus, ousting God from the throne in the process.**

Sometimes we measure our goodness, our holiness, against our spouse's, comparing our goodness to their missteps or our sins to their goodness. In both cases, we've made our spouse the judge. Sometimes we convince ourselves that if our spouse is happy, we're secure—or, on the flip side, that whenever they're unhappy, we're lost. We turn our hope from the Redeemer to the mercurial happiness of ourselves or another person, to a feeling that has no power to save or restore but that can and often does destroy.

All those people, belongings, and longings we allow to come between us and God bring heartbreak and discontent. Jesus emphasizes just how much higher and deeper than any other relationship our commitment to God must be:

> "If anyone comes to me and does not hate his own father and mother and wife and children and brothers and sisters, yes, and even his own life, he cannot be my disciple."
> LUKE 14:26

Believers must not only claim but also truly live out Jesus as Lord. Yes, He's a good master, but He is the Master. We're His servants. In far too many ways, we flip the relationship upside down in our hearts. We place ourselves in the master role, expecting Jesus to serve us. But He alone has the right and power to be on the throne.

Choosing your fiancée is the second-most-important decision of your life, and your wedding will be the second-most-important day of your life. Don't ever let this decision or your marriage come close to the importance of Jesus in your life.

The entire purpose of your life, including your marriage, is to glorify God, to point others to Jesus. Over and over, Scripture warns of the danger of not making God preeminent. When we rationalize our call to be holy as God is holy, when we compromise His truth to justify our desires, when we allow anything to gain margin over Jesus, we cheat ourselves of the joy for which He has designed us. God insists on being our only God. Jesus alone can redeem us. His Spirit alone fills us.

When we love the Creator most, we can truly enjoy and appreciate the created. Your God created you, and He created your wife so you can help each other along the journey He created for you. Keeping God first makes all the joy and beauty more meaningful. Keeping God first gives us strength and courage to face the difficulties. Keeping God first as both of you are growing closer to Him will bring you closer to each other, giving you more unity than you could ever otherwise know.

Keeping God first means choosing to pursue Him in your marriage. Keeping God first means turning to Him when you're facing a giant. Keeping God first means trusting that He has a plan when you can't see any way forward.

"I, Jesus, have sent my angel to testify to you about these things for the churches. I am the root and the descendant of David, the bright morning star." The Spirit and the Bride say, "Come."

REVELATION 22:16-17

Starting Tomorrow

Tomorrow you're marrying the one your soul loves, the woman you have chosen to share your entire life with. Your Abba, your Father, who loves you and her deeply, is joining your two lives into one—to and for His own glory. In the moment she steps into the aisle and you see her for the first time, "a bride adorned for her husband" (Revelation 21:2), everyone there will have a glimpse of how Jesus loves us, a foretaste of the day He will call us home to be with Him.

Countdown Journal

What practical steps are you taking now to be sure that everything begins and ends with Jesus?

What will you do together as a married couple to keep God at the center of your lives?

Anniversary Reflection

Take some time to reflect on and celebrate all the ways your wedding and your marriage symbolize Jesus' love for us.

How will you intentionally grow closer to God and each other as you begin your second year of a lifetime together?

Notes

DAY 14 | FORSAKE ALL OTHERS

1. "Why Is Marital Infidelity So Destructive?," GotQuestions.org, last updated August 16, 2024, https://www.gotquestions.org/marital-infidelity.html.
2. Brad Lewis, "Affairs/Marital Infidelity," Focus on the Family, February 1, 2002, https://www.focusonthefamily.com/get-help/affairs-marital-infidelity.
3. "Over Half of Practicing Christians Admit They Use Pornography," Barna Group, October 17, 2024, https://www.barna.com/trends/over-half-of-practicing-christians-admit-they-use-pornography.

DAY 10 | INVEST WISELY, STEWARD INTENTIONALLY

1. "Nearly 80% of U.S. Adults Say They're Worried About the Economy," Ramsey Solutions, October 21, 2024, https://www.ramseysolutions.com/company/newsroom/releases/Ramsey-survey-finds-majority-of-Americans-worried-about-the-economy.
2. Philip Massey, "The Parable of the Two Debtors in Modern Terms," *Chimes*, Biola University, October 27, 2010, https://chimesnewspaper.com/13189/opinions/parable-two-debtors.
3. Strong's Exhaustive Concordance "G1411—*dunamis*," accessed July 9, 2025, https://biblehub.com/greek/1411.htm.
4. Mary Fairchild, "How Heavy Was a Talent in the Bible? How Much Is a Talent of Gold?" Learn Religions, updated July 19, 2024, https://www.learnreligions.com/what-is-a-talent-700699.

DAY 9 | LOVE HER AS CHRIST LOVES THE CHURCH

1. "New Documentary Shines Light on Healthcare Responses to Violence Against Women," London School of Hygiene and Tropical Medicine, April 10, 2025, https://www.lshtm.ac.uk/newsevents/news/2025/new-documentary-shines-light-healthcare-responses-violence-against-women.
2. UNICEF, *Hidden in Plain Sight: A Statistical Analysis of Violence Against*

Children (September 2014), https://data.unicef.org/resources/hidden-in-plain-sight-a-statistical-analysis-of-violence-against-children.

3. UNODC Research and Trend Analysis Branch, *Global Study on Homicide 2013: Trends, Contexts, Data* (UNODC, 2013), 14, https://www.unodc.org/documents/gsh/pdfs/2014_GLOBAL_HOMICIDE_BOOK_web.pdf.
4. "Female Genital Mutilation: A Global Concern," UNICEF, March 7, 2024, https://data.unicef.org/resources/female-genital-mutilation-a-global-concern-2024.

DAY 8 | REJOICE! (STEP 1 FOR FIGHTING WELL)

1. *Merriam-Webster*, "rejoice (*v.*)," accessed June 1, 2025, https://www.merriam-webster.com/dictionary/rejoice.

DAY 7 | AIM FOR RESTORATION (STEP 2 FOR FIGHTING WELL)

1. *Merriam-Webster*, "aim (*v.*)," accessed August 14, 2025, https://www.merriam-webster.com/dictionary/aim.

DAY 6 | COMFORT EACH OTHER (STEP 3 FOR FIGHTING WELL)

1. John Bechtle, "*Parakaleo*—Ministry to the Stuck: Greek Word of the Week," Ezra Project, January 2, 2021, https://ezraproject.com/parakaleo-ministry-to-the-stuck.

DAY 5 | AGREE WITH EACH OTHER (STEP 4 FOR FIGHTING WELL)

1. "Strong's G846—*autos*," Blue Letter Bible, accessed June 27, 2025, https://www.blueletterbible.org/lexicon/g846/kjv/tr/0-1.
2. "Strong's G5426—*phroneō*," Blue Letter Bible, accessed June 27, 2025, https://www.blueletterbible.org/lexicon/g5426/kjv/tr/0-1.

DAY 3 | COMMIT TO DAILY AFFECTION

1. "Strong's G782—*aspazomai*," Blue Letter Bible, accessed August 14, 2025, https://www.blueletterbible.org/lexicon/g782/esv/mgnt/0-1.
2. Susan Krauss Whitbourne, "The Kiss of Health," *Fulfillment at Any Age* (blog), *Psychology Today*, July 24, 2012, https://www.psychologytoday.com/blog/fulfillment-any-age/201207/the-kiss-health.
3. Whitbourne, "Kiss of Health."
4. Stacey Colino, "The Health Benefits of Hugging," *U.S. News & World Report*, February 3, 2016, https://health.usnews.com/health-news/health-wellness/articles/2016-02-03/the-health-benefits-of-hugging.
5. The quiz is available at Love Languages, accessed June 27, 2025, https://5lovelanguages.com/quizzes/love-language.
6. Robert Herrick, "To Anthea. (III)," *The Works of Robert Herrick*, vol. 1, ed. Alfred Pollard (1891; Luminarium, 2009), https://www.luminarium.org/sevenlit/herrick/toanthea3.htm.

7. Quoted at Melissa Barnhart, "*Duck Dynasty*'s Si Robertson on Life, Marriage Proposals, and His Unwavering Belief in the Creator," The Christian Post, September 1, 2013, https://www.christianpost.com/news/interview-duck-dynastys-si-robertson-on-life-marriage-proposals-and-his-unwavering-belief-in-the-creator.html.

DAY 2 | CELEBRATE SEX

1. Jimmy Evans, "How to Transform Your Marriage with a Vision Retreat," XO Marriage, accessed June 1, 2025, https://xomarriage.com/articles/how-to-transform-your-marriage-with-a-vision-retreat.
2. Ellen Frank et al., "Frequency of Sexual Dysfunction in 'Normal' Couples," *The New England Journal of Medicine* 299, no. 3 (1978): 111–15, https://doi.org/10.1056/NEJM197807202990302.
3. Allen B. Mallory, "Dimensions of Couples' Sexual Communication, Relationship Satisfaction, and Sexual Satisfaction: A Meta-Analysis," *Journal of Family Psychology*, 36 no. 3 (2021): 358–71, https://pmc.ncbi.nlm.nih.gov/articles/PMC9153093.
4. Kyle D. Killian, "Sexual Desire Discrepancy: Why It's a Big Deal for Couples," *Intersections* (blog), *Psychology Today*, December 27, 2019, https://www.psychologytoday.com/us/blog/intersections/201912/sexual-desire-discrepancy-why-it-s-big-deal-couples.
5. Brian D. Doss et al., "The Effect of the Transition to Parenthood on Relationship Quality: An 8-Year Prospective Study," *Journal of Personality and Social Psychology* 96, no. 3 (2009): 601–19, https://doi.org/10.1037/a0013969.
6. Kristen P. Mark et al., "Infidelity in Heterosexual Couples: Demographic, Interpersonal, and Personality-Related Predictors of Extradyadic Sex," *Archives of Sexual Behavior* 40 (2011): 971–82, https://doi.org/10.1007/s10508-011-9771-z.
7. Raymond C. Rosen, "Prevalence and Risk Factors of Sexual Dysfunction in Men and Women," *Current Psychiatry Reports* 2, no. 3 (2000): 189–95, https://doi.org/10.1007/s11920-996-0006-2.
8. "Do Mental Health Problems Have an Effect on Sexual Function?," International Society for Sexual Medicine, accessed March 25, 2025, https://www.issm.info/sexual-health-qa/do-mental-health-problems-have-an-effect-on-sexual-function.

DAY 1 | BEGIN AND END EVERYTHING WITH JESUS

1. Leann Murphy (Karen Leann Murphy) (@karenleannroseberrymurphy), "One month in our new home," Facebook, December 16, 2023, https://www.facebook.com/share/v/1ArVbfJQXi.